L E S S O N S
from
NEBRASKA
FOOTBALL

LESSONS FROM NEBRASKA FOOTBALL

Gordon Thiessen and Mark Todd, Lessons from Nebraska Football

ISBN 1-887002-98-7

Cross Training Publishing
317 West Second Street
Grand Island, NE 68801
(800) 430-8588

This book is manufactured in the United States of America.

Library of Congress Cataloging in Publication Data in Progress.

Published by Cross Training Publishing
317 West Second Street
Grand Island, NE 68801
1-800-430-8588

Cover Credit:
© Lynda Lambrecht Stych

"I can do all things through Christ who strengthens me."
–Philippians 4:13 (NKJV)

CONTENTS

INTRODUCTION

I once remember a high school football player explaining to me that satanic music and images brought out his greatest "field character": aggression, anger, hate, revenge—attributes that many feel are necessary to excel in a sport like football. Perhaps most would not resort to what they would refer to as satanic methods to produce football energy, but quite a number of us Christians have bought into the notion that we must put our faith on hold while we engage in sports. In other words, "separation of church and state" has not only haunted Christians in public schools, but on the athletic gridiron as well.

Colossians 1:16b states that "all things were created by Him and for Him [Christ]."

Jesus Christ and our faith in Him is relevant in every area of our lives, including athletics. In fact, God desires an "offensive-proactive" mentality with athletics. Athletic and coaching ability are weapons from God to aggressively bring Him honor, glory, and victory. God desires to sharpen these weapons and to train us for the battle by developing our character to appropriately use them.

Squeezing God out of the athletic equation brings about temporary results at best. God has so much more to offer in terms of fulfillment, maximization of ability, and eternal value for the athlete, coach, and even fans as we seek Him for the golden nuggets of character.

In my Christian walk in sports, I've known God to be a great "Athletic Director" as He sets my schedule and selects my opponents to test and try me—further opportunity for character development. God has been my great "Equipment Manager," providing the necessary protection that I need for every "showdown" to keep me so I may do His will. God has been a wonderful "Medical Trainer." He has healed and rehabilitated my broken heart and dreams one by one through the aggressive game of life.

I've truly known my Heavenly Father to be the Great Player-Coach. Not only does He develop my skills through study of His playbook (the Bible) and daily communication in prayer, but He also has set the sacrificial example of performance as the Greatest Player of all: Jesus.

Lessons from Nebraska Football will serve as a useful tool for athletes, coaches, and fans to see how wonderfully relevant God has been, not only to Nebraska football but sports as a whole. After reading these inspirational stories, you'll begin to see God scoring eternal touchdowns through your life.

Ron Brown
Receivers Coach, University of Nebraska

FOREWORD

Over the years, I have become more and more convinced that attitude, chemistry, and unity are issues that play a critical role in determining the success of athletic teams. I have been fortunate to know many people of faith during my 36-year coaching career at Nebraska. Gordon Thiessen and Mark Todd have collected the stories of many of those athletes and have also included many of the moments in recent Nebraska football history that relate to issues of faith. Gordon and Mark have done an excellent job of relating personal stories and events to the Scriptures. Their analogies are excellent and can be applied to almost any life situation.

In a time when it seems as though issues of faith and character have become progressively less important to our culture, the authors illustrate the life-changing aspects of Christianity and a personal faith in Jesus. The factor that most convinced me of the reality of God's presence as revealed in Jesus has been the dramatic changes I have observed in the lives of so many players and coaches. These changes would not have occurred if there was not an authentic transforming power to the Christian faith.

I recommend this book to those who are seeking guidance in their spiritual life. I particularly recommend it to young people who are looking for people with whom they can identify in a world where there are increasingly fewer role models to follow.

Tom Osborne
Former Head Coach, University of Nebraska

LESSON ONE

Players Unite in Prayer

The late November scenario of that intense rivalry was all too familiar. Over 76,000 screaming fans filled the stands in Lincoln's Memorial Stadium. Both teams were ranked inside the top five, and the Big Eight Championship and a trip to the Orange Bowl were on the line. Barry Switzer stood on the sideline opposite Tom Osborne. It was them versus us.

The sight seemed unlikely, even as it happened. Yet, on Nov. 22, 1986, about a dozen Nebraska and Oklahoma players huddled at midfield before kick-off to pray. Some kneeled, others stood hand-in-hand.

For former Nebraska offensive guard and team captain Stan Parker, that mental image from his senior season has engraved itself within his memory. It has represented his life perspective—viewing his existence in light of eternity. With his football career's biggest game at hand, he gathered with rival players to worship God. Though that game was big at the time, its significance has faded over the years. However, their example of public prayer during competition has lasted. Now it is common for teams to meet following a football game and unite in prayer.

See what the Bible has to say about things that will fade away. "The brother in humble circumstances ought to take pride in his high position. But the one who is rich should take pride in his low position because he will pass away like a wild flower. For the sun rises with scorching heat and withers the plant; its blossom falls and its beauty is destroyed. In the same ways the rich man will fade away even while he goes about his business" (James 1:9-11).

Do you spend too much time thinking about things that will fade? The Bible teaches that social status, material wealth, and power mean nothing to God. While this world may be impressed by each of these areas and even honor us for them, each will fade.

Believe it or not, all the big games and national championships will someday mean very little to future sports fans. Sadly, people live with an insatiable desire for on-field success, demanding, "What have you done for me lately?" At first, it may not seem so obvious as to how great sports moments are fading in brilliance. But, for example, how many fans still wear jerseys commemorating Johnny Rodgers or Jerry Tagge from the great Cornhusker national championship teams of the early 1970s?

It's been said that few people on their death bed will be glad they spent extra time working at the office. Instead, most will wish they spent more time investing in the lives of others or developing their relationship with God. How can you begin to spend less time on things that fade and more time on things that last?

First, decide what is really important in life. You can start by defining what success is from God's perspective. Don't listen to what others use to define success. Most of their definitions will include things that will fade. Success is not so much a destination as it is a lifestyle. "Whatever you do, work at it with all your heart, as working for the Lord, not for men" (Colossians 3:23).

Ask yourself if you are reaching toward a goal to achieve a destination or to live your life for Christ. Do you picture Him as your audience, or are you more concerned with pleasing others? Make a list of the things that are most important to you. Then ask yourself, "What is going to last?"

Second, stop spending time on things that aren't really important. The Apostle Paul put it this way: "Be very careful, then, how you live—not as unwise but as wise, making the most of every opportunity because the days are evil" (Ephesians 5:15-16). Paul was trying to stress the urgency of keeping our standards high and making wise decisions. Spending too much time in front of the television may be fun, but it may also be a poor use of our time. When you're tempted to stay up late watching a TV show, ask yourself, "Tomorrow morning when I get up, will I be glad that I stayed up an extra half-hour to watch TV (or play video games)?"

Everything you do is influenced by what you think is important. Take some time this week to make sure you're not placing too much importance on things that will fade.

LESSON TWO

Huskers Adopt New Attitude

The 1993 Cornhusker football team emerged from spring practice with a new attitude. Jan. 1, 1993, marked a 27-14 Orange Bowl loss to third-ranked Florida State. It was Nebraska's sixth straight bowl loss, but it served as a springboard, as the program went on to dominate the 1990s by playing in four national title games and winning three championships. Following the April '93 intrasquad scrimmage, Tommie Frazier stated his heartfelt passion for the team.

"I think we're capable of winning it all next year," Frazier stated. "It's just up to us to go out and play consistently and not have any lapses."

The team later adopted the slogan, "We refuse to lose."

Nine months later, on Jan. 1, 1994, No. 2 Nebraska trailed the top-ranked Seminoles by a deuce following a Florida State field goal with 21 seconds remaining. Though time was waning, Husker players did not lose heart. On the ensuing drive, sophomore quarterback Frazier completed a 29-yard pass to tight end Trumane Bell inside the Florida State 30 with one second remaining. On the next play, NU kicker Byron Bennett's field goal attempt sailed wide left. Cornhusker players left the field saddened, but proud.

"I feel like we're still champions," stated Nebraska All-American linebacker Trev Alberts. "There's not a frown on my face."

Players on the 1993 Nebraska football team rekindled a passion for winning. Their "refuse to lose" mentality eventually propelled the program to three national titles in the 1990s.

While our zest for sports may be important, it's not nearly as important as the enthusiasm needed to serve our God. Here is how the Bible describes one church's lack of enthusiasm: "I know your deeds, that you are neither cold nor hot. I wish you were either one or the other! So, because you are lukewarm—neither hot nor cold—I am about to spit you out of my mouth. You say, 'I am rich; I have acquired wealth and do not need a thing.' But you do not realize that you are wretched, pitiful, poor, blind and naked" (Revelation 3:15-17).

The Apostle John was chewing out the Church in Laodicea in this passage because they had lost their zest to serve God. Laodicea was a wealthy city known for its banking and industry. But in spite of its great wealth, it had a problem with its water supply. The aqueduct that was built to bring water to the city from the hot springs didn't work properly. By the time the water reached the city, it was neither hot nor refreshingly cool—only lukewarm. John's point was that the city had become as bland about its faith as the water that came into the city.

Are you hot or cold when it comes to serving God? Is your faith lukewarm? Think about it when you drink lukewarm water—yuck! Do you remember the practices or games when you were dying to take a drink of water? Lukewarm water just didn't cut it. And neither does the faith of someone who is a halfhearted, in-name-only Christian who relies on his or her own talent and ability.

Don't follow God halfway. Commit yourself to letting God rekindle your faith and get you into the game. If you find yourself following God halfway, ask yourself, "How does my level of earthly wealth affect my spiritual desire?" Earthly wealth had become so important to the Laodiceans that what they could see and buy had become more important to them than the spiritual wealth that is unseen and eternal. Let me put it this way: If a major league baseball player becomes more focused on salary negotiations than glorifying God, he will begin to lose his zest for serving Him. The riches that count are the riches that are in Christ.

Decide to take a stand for your faith. If you don't do anything for God, the tendency is to become lazy and indifferent toward your faith. Here is advice from the Apostle Paul about taking a stand for God: "Therefore, my dear brothers, stand firm. Let nothing move you. Always give yourselves fully to the work of the Lord because you know that your labor in the Lord is not in vain" (1 Corinthians 15:58).

God doesn't want someone going half-speed for Him any more than a coach wants his team to play a game at half-speed. Don't hold back. You've got every reason to be fired up to serve God!

LESSON THREE

The wait is over. The euphoric cheers and synchronized clapping of 76,000 fans are so loudly mingled with the music of Alan Parsons Project that the electric atmosphere is almost silent. A giant television screen draws the crowd's attention as the tunnel walk unfolds. Gladiators in red march from their south stadium locker room to the edge of the football field at Nebraska's Memorial Stadium. Then, on cue, players and coaches dart to their east sideline, trailing ecstatic banner-waving and back-flipping Husker cheerleaders. The crowd erupts. It's game time!

The Cornhusker football team's tunnel walk is a moment of pride and celebration as players and coaches charge onto the field with great fanfare. For those fans, it's always fun to see their team return to action. For all of us who are committed to Jesus Christ, we know the Lord will make the ultimate return. There won't be any press conferences to announce His return. But we do know that our Savior will keep His promise. He clearly announced that He would one day make His return and it would come quickly (Revelation 22:12).

While fans anxiously await the tunnel walk at Nebraska's Memorial Stadium, it can't begin to compare to the excitement when Jesus returns to earth.

"Look, He is coming with the clouds, and every eye

will see Him, even those who pierced Him; and all the people of the earth will mourn because of Him. So shall it be! Amen" (Revelation 1:7). It will be the greatest moment in history since His return to heaven. For those who have rejected Him, it will be bitter disappointment and despair. But for those who have received Him and await His return, it will bring joy and hope.

Do you look forward to His return? The promise of Jesus' return isn't remote or a good possibility—it's definite. And this promise should give us hope and strength.

Are you prepared for the Lord's return? Here are a couple of thoughts on the greatest arrival that the world will ever witness.

Fear not! Don't doubt for a moment that you are secure in God's love. His promises are sound and His return is definite. In 1 Thessalonians 4:13-5:2, the Apostle Paul writes to the Thessalonian Christians about the Lord's return. Verses 16-17 read, "For the Lord Himself will come down from heaven with a loud command, with the voice of the archangel, and with the trumpet call of God, and the dead in Christ will rise first. After that, we who are still alive and are left will be caught up together with them in the clouds to meet the Lord in the air. And so we will be with the Lord forever."

"Fear not!" needs to be our attitude toward life. Verses 13 and 14 read, "We do not want you to be ignorant . . . or grieve like the rest of men, who have no hope. We believe that Jesus died and rose again, and so we believe that God will bring with Jesus those who have fallen asleep [passed away] in Him." Verse 18 within the same chapter states, "Therefore, encourage each other with these words." We have a reason to live in hope and need to share this truth with others. Death is not the end, nor are the defeats and failures of this life final. It shouldn't matter if we face the greatest challenge of our lives on or off the playing field. There is nothing to fear with Christ our Savior.

Plan for tomorrow, but live like Christ will return today. First Thessalonians chapter 5 talks about preparing for the Lord's return. It explains how vital it is to live for the Lord and not for the passing pleasures of this world. Think about this: If you had the opportunity to meet your favorite sports hero tomorrow morning, how would you prepare? Would you clean your house if he or she were coming to dinner? Would you think about what you might say and do? How about the Lord's Second Coming to earth? How would you live your life differently today, knowing He might come at any moment? Would it influence the way you treat your friends and family? Don't take anything for granted. He never told us how soon He would return, but the fact that He will return should encourage us to live godly lives. Remember that Jesus Christ is the greatest! Take time to appreciate Him and His promise to return.

LESSON FOUR

Osborne Criticized

For the Nebraska football program, 1995 marked a year that featured perhaps the greatest team ever assembled, as it dominated all opponents during its 12-0 national title campaign. But for Coach Osborne, it was a time of great tension as he sought to do the right thing amidst controversies involving a small handful of players who had allegedly broken the law.

One such player was leading Heisman Trophy candidate running back Lawrence Phillips. According to Lancaster County Court documents, Phillips was charged with assault, trespass, and destruction of property relating to an incident involving his former girlfriend on Sept. 10, 1995. The destruction of property charge was later dropped by the State. However, Phillips was convicted of the other charges with a plea of no contest.

Phillips, initially suspended from the team indefinitely, was reinstated six games later after Osborne decided that he responded well to counseling. Osborne said he felt the structure and stability of football was important to Phillips' life toward a hopeful recovery from his behavioral problem. With that decision to reinstate Phillips, Osborne's reputation was on the line. Many criticized him for his decision, saying he was a win-at-all-costs coach.

Osborne responded, "Some people believe that the way the Lawrence Phillips thing was handled was absolutely wrong. It sent the wrong message. It was not proper. And a lot of people who know I'm a Christian were probably turned off. But through that situation, some people began to see that God is a God of second chances, that every person is acceptable in His sight. No one can do anything so bad that we are cut off from His love and acceptance. And maybe there was a redeeming sense in this whole thing. I'm not asking people to say what I did was right or wrong. I don't know for sure what was right or wrong."

As he admittedly struggled to search for the best means of handling the situation, Osborne said he spent a lot of time in prayer and reading the Bible.

Tom Osborne knew he would be criticized for his decision regarding Phillips. Though the Husker coach admitted he didn't know if he had done the right thing regarding that player, he indicated that his ultimate desire was to do the right thing, to the best of his knowledge. And though he was labeled by some as a win-at-all-costs coach, Osborne's reputation for fairness and honesty remained amidst that controversial decision.

The Bible is clear when it comes to the value of our reputation. "A good name is more desirable than great riches; to be esteemed is better than silver or gold" (Proverbs 22:1).

Whether you are an athlete, coach, or businessman, your reputation is much more valuable than you might think. And while each of us is probably not under the scrutiny of the public eye like a football coach, God does see all we do and say. Although our position in Christ is not in jeopardy when we blow it, our mistakes do grieve the God we serve. Thankfully, we serve a forgiving God.

Reputation is who people think we are, and character is who we actually are. What we think about Tom Osborne is not nearly as important as his true character. We'll look at the importance of character later. Yet, reputation does matter. God may be more concerned with character, but reputation is important to any football program, school, or business. It doesn't take much to ruin a good reputation—a slip of the tongue or a temper that goes unchecked could do it. What can we do to protect not only our reputation, but more importantly, God's reputation?

First, don't put yourself in any situation that might compromise your reputation. Joseph is an example of someone who made sure he removed himself from a compromising situation. "Now Joseph was handsome in form and appearance. And it came about after these events that his master's wife looked with desire at Joseph, and she said, 'Lie with me' . . . And he left his garment in her hand and fled and went outside" (Genesis 39:1-12). He ran like mad and never looked back.

Second, join an accountability team. Maybe it's a friend or your Bible study group. The Bible is clear in Ecclesiastes 4:9, "Two are better than one because they have a good return for their work." *The Living Bible* puts it this way: "The results can be much better." There is a lot to gain by having someone hold us accountable to God's standards of conduct. They can help us gain and keep perspective. They can provide valuable objectivity. Sometimes just getting their input can make the difference between compromise and sticking to our principles.

LESSON FIVE

Character Counts For Osborne

When people reflect on the highlights of Tom Osborne's 255-win, 25-year head coaching career, they often think in terms of big games and three national championships.

Though Osborne remembers those events, he places more value on the process behind those games and seasons. Fans remember the numbers, but Osborne remembers the players and coaches and their commitment to excellence. For Osborne, playing by the rules and maximizing the team's potential were basic requirements.

"Sometimes you don't win the trophy," he said. "But your performance is what counts, and tenacity and maximizing your abilities and those kinds of things are really more critical."

Competing with character was everything.

Character counts, no doubt about it. But what is character? Is it only the ability to perform when the odds are against you? Or is it much more? Here are some thoughts about character:

"The highest reward for a man's toil is not what he gets for it, but rather what he becomes by it."
—*American Way*

"God is more concerned about our character than our

comfort. His goal is not to pamper us physically, but to perfect us spiritually." —Paul W. Powell

"Only what we have wrought into our character during life can we take with us." —Humboldt

"Sow a thought, reap an act; sow an act, reap a habit; sow a habit, reap a character; sow a character, reap a destiny."

"Character is what we do when no one else is looking."

Character is a word that is used only a few times in the Bible. It's a word that is rarely used or shown on prime time TV, yet we recognize it when we see it. Most people define character by the lack of it. They look around at the moral collapse in our society and point to examples of cheating, lying and drug abuse and know that we lack character. Many feel like they're sinking in the quicksand of immoral behavior.

Character is the person God sees when He looks at us, and it's not always the same person that our closest friends see. "God sees not as man sees, for man looks at the outward appearance, but the Lord looks at the heart" (1 Samuel 16:7).

Now, let's face it. Though we as Christians are forgiven and spotless in God's eyes, by no means have we reached perfection. Through trials and life's lessons, God is working to chip away our character flaws like a jeweler crafts a diamond. It's important as we live our lives that our greatest concern should be for godly character development. It often involves a change of lifestyle. It often means a consistent adjustment in our attitudes and actions. In short, spiritual growth and character development occur when God's Word makes a practical and positive change in the way we live our lives.

Be a doer of God's Word. Don't rely on church attendance, being busy for God, or education for spiritual growth. It's not only knowing the right stuff, but rather doing the right things that produces character. "Do not merely listen to the word, and so deceive yourselves. Do what it says" (James 1:22).

Live a Christlike life so that others might be inspired to do what is right. We need men and women who are ready to lead by example (Matthew 5:16).

LESSON SIX

Crouch Accepts Role

He entered the 1998 football season with Nebraska as the backup quarterback. Redshirt freshman Eric Crouch was a competitor at heart and frustrated at first that he didn't make the grade to start. Nevertheless, he accepted a team supporting role. Following a knee injury to starter sophomore Bobby Newcombe inflicted during the season opener, however, Crouch found himself playing lead during most of the season.

"There's definitely a big role in being a team player," Crouch said at the conclusion of the regular season. "In terms of the things I've done on this team, I've never looked at it on a personal level at all. Going into the season, I knew that I was going to be the backup, and that was going to be my role for the year. But I also thought that being a backup here at Nebraska probably isn't the worst thing in the world. I'm probably going to play a lot and gain a lot of experience. There was a point in time when all my dreams and my aspirations were to be the first-string quarterback—to do all these other things and to be 'the man.' That's not what happened, but I stuck with it. And unfortunately, someone gets hurt, and I'm the next guy who goes in. I've learned a lot from it, and I'm real thankful I've been given this opportunity. Right now I probably couldn't ask for much more."

What one-word description comes to mind when you think of how Eric Crouch carried himself when he was named the backup quarterback and later the starter? What about "unselfish"? His response was refreshing, since many athletes struggle with self-centeredness, and recognition is often at the heart of competition. Former NBA San Antonio Spurs coach Bob Hill put it this way: "I think a lot of these kids today are the products of no discipline in schools. When we were in school, if we did something wrong, we'd be disciplined. Today, none of that happens. Now you've got these young guys who went to school with no discipline. Then they get recruited to play basketball in college, and they get paid. Then they come out of school early and expect to make millions of dollars in the NBA."

Whether it's a lack of discipline at school or home, ego and self-centeredness are at the heart of the problem. But these problems are not exclusive to athletes. In fact, even Jesus' disciples struggled with their own selfish ambitions of being the greatest in God's kingdom. When the disciples argued over who should be number one, Jesus taught His men an important truth about ego: "They came to Capernaum. When He was in the house, He asked them, 'What were you arguing about on the road?' But they kept quiet because on the way they had argued about whom was the greatest. Sitting down, Jesus called the Twelve and said, 'If anyone wants to be first, he must be the very last and the servant of all'" (Mark 9:33-35).

In sports, greatness is often defined by status: the number of games won, an MVP award, a championship trophy, or the size of your contract. But God determines greatness in His kingdom by service, not status. Jesus' disciples failed to grasp God's view of greatness. The phrase "he must be the very last" describes putting another person's interests ahead of your own. So, if you want to be great in God's eyes, put the emphasis on others rather than drawing attention to yourself.

Compare your motives with Christ's. It's not easy to compare our motives to Christ's. That's why the disciples were afraid to answer Jesus' questions. They were wrapped up in their own personal success and were embarrassed to answer His questions. It's not wrong to be ambitious, but when ambition becomes more important than obedience, it becomes sin. Pride can often cause us to overvalue our position or rewards from sports or other areas of life. Compare your motives with Christ's, and choose His way, not the world's.

Become great by putting other people ahead of your own interests. If you really want to be great, then do your best to serve others. Eric Crouch recognized the importance of being a team player. On God's team, it not only serves the best interests of the team, but God commands us to be great by serving others.

LESSON SEVEN

Osborne Perseveres

Throughout most of his 25-year Nebraska football head coaching career, Tom Osborne was criticized by many fans and members of the national media. They claimed he couldn't win the big one—whether the "big one" meant beating some of Barry Switzer's Oklahoma teams of the 1970s and '80s or by winning the national championship. But critics could not find fault in Osborne's nine-plus win seasons, the consecutive bowl trips, the consistent national rankings, the academic success of many student athletes, and his character in general.

"All I can do is be consistent and faithful, then hopefully that might bear some positive fruit," Osborne said a season prior to winning his first of three national titles. "I live in a very unstable world of athletics where if you base your security on the win-loss record or the job that you have or whatever, you're certainly in a roller-coaster existence—when you win, you're a great coach in the eyes of other people, but when you lose, you're a bum. It's a pretty hard way to live. I think if you're anchored in Christianity, there's a certain stability to your life that is not dependent entirely on external circumstances."

All people go through periods of struggle and slumps in their lives. But as Tom Osborne illustrated, one has to persevere through them with a proper perspective. Osborne also saw the importance of accepting responsibility and not blaming others when persevering through tough situations.

Have you heard anyone this week blame someone else for his/her own problems? A kicker for the Dallas Cowboys was once asked why he missed a field goal in a game against the Houston Oilers. "I was too busy reading my stats on the scoreboard." Then when he later missed another one, he said the stadium's grass was "too tall." Yet, in another game he said, "My helmet was too tight and it was squeezing my brain." Once he even blamed the holder for placing the ball upside down.

While you and I might laugh at this example, we've all made excuses for a poor performance or a bad attitude. How does a Christian work through a slump? Let's begin by recognizing that your thoughts control your actions. If you want to change the way you hit, you must first change how you think. Psychology discovered this truth in the last century, but Solomon taught this principle thousands of years earlier. "Be careful how you think; your life is shaped by your thoughts" (Proverbs 4:23, Good News Bible). Here are four guidelines for changing the way you think about any slump:

1. **Put your trust in God.** According to Proverbs 3:5-6 and other passages, you should put your trust in God and depend on Him. You can choose to rely on yourself, but doesn't it make more sense to place your faith in the One who created you? Just as a head coach is the best person to direct his team, in a similar way, God is in the best position to guide you through your slumps.

2. **Pray and believe God is sufficient.** In the words of the Apostle Paul from Philippians 4:6-7, we are to pray about all of our circumstances. "Do not be anxious about

anything, but in everything, by prayer and petition, with thanksgiving, present your requests to God. And the peace of God, which transcends all understanding, will guard your hearts and minds in Christ Jesus."

Whatever your request is, do you regularly and diligently bring it to God in prayer, trusting that He will help you? If not, why not? God is able.

The Bible says it over and over. "Do you not know? Have you not heard? The Lord is the everlasting God, the Creator of the ends of the earth. He will not grow tired or weary" (Isaiah 40:28). He is able to control nature, alter circumstances, and change people.

3. Choose to be joyful. Happiness depends on circumstances, but we can experience joy in spite of a slump. Outlook determines outcome, and attitude determines action. A joyful attitude is essential when working through a slump. James says, "Consider it pure joy, my brothers whenever you face trials of many kinds" (James 1:2).

4. Forget the past; focus on the goal. You must learn from the past, but do not be controlled by it. Any runner who looks backward while running forward risks losing the race. The Apostle Paul gives several ways to apply this truth. "Brothers, I do not consider myself yet to have taken hold of it. But one thing I do: Forgetting what is behind and straining toward what is ahead, I press on toward the goal to win the prize for which God has called me heavenward in Christ Jesus" (Philippians 3:13-14).

LESSON EIGHT

Champs Focus on Repeat

Husker players entered the 1995 season with a national title under their belts and a hunger for another. The team knew they possessed the top-quality athletes it would take to win. They knew that unity on and off the field were critical. They knew the coaching staff offered the best conditioning, practice, and game plans and that they had to follow those steps if they wanted to be in position for a repeat championship. And thus, on January 2, 1996, Nebraska was once again poised for another national crown.

The Fiesta Bowl was hyped as a dogfight with No. 1 Nebraska's bulldozing ground attack against the high-speed aerial assault of No. 2 Florida's fun-and-gun offense. The final score, 62-24, may have been a surprise to fans and media, but not to the victorious Huskers. As a unit they were not arrogant, simply confident and well-prepared.

"That just shows when you practice well, you play well," explained former NU defensive captain Tony Veland following the blowout. "Have faith in your coaches. They know what they are doing. We knew we had good athletes to go along with theirs. If we played our coverages and our responsibilities, we knew there weren't too many things that were going to hurt us, regardless of their athletes."

The 1996 Fiesta Bowl national championship was a blowout, but it probably would have been dramatically different had the players not prepared well or followed through with the game plan. Preparation to win that

LESSON NINE

Coach Stresses Unity

Though the civil rights movement has championed the cause of preventing racial discrimination, we still live in a world of great racial tension. Nebraska receivers' coach Ron Brown, who serves as a Fellowship of Christian Athletes national spokesman for racial reconciliation, frequently expresses his heartfelt passion for this cause. Brown often challenges Christians to live in racial harmony as a product of right Christian living.

"So many times, when it comes to the issue of race relations, we are taught to divide and hate," Brown said on a Christian radio program. "Someone came along in my life and taught me that this is wrong. She demonstrated by her actions that love is the only answer."

Brown's desire for race reconciliation arose from the example of a middle-aged benefactor he remembers, the late Mrs. Chinland.

"She was a wealthy white board member of an inner-city orphanage, consisting primarily of black and Hispanic children,"
he explained. "I was one of those children, and she saw to it that I was adopted by a loving couple. She went above and beyond the call of duty."

While Brown was growing up, she regularly sent him birthday cards with money inside. Mrs. Chinland later even funded a portion of his graduate school tuition. Her example has burned in his heart when surrounded by circumstances that might have motivated him to be racially divisive. Brown recalled a high school football coach who attempted to incite racial hatred to inspire player performance.

"He once suggested that we remember history and slavery and the oppression of blacks across the world. In this instance, he tried to teach us how to hate so we would play better. But it became very difficult to hate as I continually thought about Mrs. Chinland."

In spite of the racial tensions he's witnessed in life, Coach Brown has sought to live in light of the example of Mrs. Chinland.

Reconciliation is greatly needed among the different races in our society. I believe there are three types of people when it comes to racial reconciliation: accusers, excusers, and choosers.

Accusers will blame others for everything. Applied to race reconciliation, some white people might blame their problems on Affirmative Action programs and say things like, "Blacks act like we [whites] owe them some special favors because of something we had nothing to do with." On the other side, some blacks accuse whites of refusing to give them opportunities because of the color of their skin. "That guy didn't even consider me for the promotion because I'm black!"

While excusers don't always play the blame game, they do have an excuse for everything. George Washington Carver said, "Ninety-nine percent of all failures come from people who've perfected the habit of making excuses." When it comes to race issues, it's easy to blame others for our circumstances (economics) or background (environment). But each time we make excuses for our behavior, we move further away from the solution. When whites are asked why they don't do something about racism, some will say, "I don't know any blacks, and besides, a lot of them are doing okay today." When blacks are asked the same question, some will say, "They [whites] don't have any idea what we've been through—they just don't understand us."

The Apostle Paul realized that neither the accuser nor excuser view is biblical. We need to be a chooser. It's up to us to choose to be a part of racial reconciliation. Paul and his co-worker, Barnabas, had worked hard to bring together two groups of people in Antioch: Jews and

Gentiles. Antioch was the first true multiracial church. This early church became the base of operation for Paul and Barnabas.

This multiracial team of believers made an impact on others because they refused to accuse or excuse racial separation. The choices they faced were no different than the choices we have today. We can choose to disagree with one another and split along racial lines. But the result will be two different churches. It's been said that the most segregated time in America is Sunday morning at church. Even though we may agree to disagree rather than confront our differences, we will still remain two separate groups.

God's choice for us is unity built through communication and conflict resolution. It may be a fight, but it's a battle that's worth fighting. Paul fought for unity in 1 Corinthians 1:10: "I appeal to you, brothers, in the name of our Lord Jesus Christ, that all of you agree with one another so that there may be no divisions among you and that you may be perfectly united in mind and thought."

All of us need to confess racial prejudice. Our responsibility is to choose to be a reconciler like the Apostle Paul. The early church struggled with reconciliation, but eventually it became one body—Jew, Greek, Samaritan, and Gentile—proving that God can bring races together. Choose to be the type of person that God can use to bring unity to the body of Christ. After all, someday we will spend eternity together. Isn't it about time we met our future teammates?

LESSON TEN

Former Player Transformed

"I was an alcoholic," admitted former Nebraska All-American tight end Junior Miller.

Life for college football's best tight end in 1979 and eventual NFL Pro Bowl receiver appeared beyond hope as he sat alone contemplating suicide.

"I believed in God, but I never really took time to search Him out. I thought I was successful, but I was becoming a failure with my marriage. I spent all my time at the lake drinking. I believe there were a lot of people praying for Junior Miller.

"I started to cry because I thought I was losing control of myself. And I just yelled out for Jesus. 'Jesus, come into my life!'"

The change in Junior was miraculous.

"I was sincere in my heart. And all I know is that the minute that I said those words, it was done. The battle was over. I wasn't drunk anymore. I was an alcoholic, and I had been smoking six or seven packs of cigarettes a day. But I haven't had a drink or cigarette since then. I truly became a born-again person because I know that Junior Miller didn't change himself. I know God changed me!"

That newness of life was incredibly evident to one of his former college drinking buddies. One day Junior, the hulking former Pro Bowl receiver, stood along the Cornhusker sideline during a practice. His large hands on his waist, Junior's bright, friendly eyes widened as he turned to see a friend from his college days of alcohol and marijuana approach. The change in Miller's heart was evident before he said a word to the newcomer.

"Junior!" the friend exclaimed. "You changed!"

"What are you talking about?" Miller replied with a grin as he shook his hand.

"You look so . . . clean."

"That's the Lord!" Miller beamed sincerely.

"A lot of my old friends have met me and talked to me since," Junior reflected with a smile. "Strangely enough, they don't like being around me because I'm not the same guy. And a lot of them notice it right away—the minute they see me, even before I open my mouth."

Yes, the change in Junior Miller was obvious to his old friends. Junior's testimony demonstrates how no one is beyond God's miraculous saving grace. God's power through our unselfish prayers can never be over-emphasized.

Prior to accepting Christ, Junior described himself as a self-serving alcoholic and the life of the party. Personal glory and self-satisfaction consumed his heart prior to his conversion. He was a consensus All-American tight end in 1979. He played seven seasons in the NFL with Atlanta and New Orleans. Following the 1980 and '81 seasons, he was selected for the Pro Bowl. Junior Miller had enjoyed phenomenal success as both a collegiate and a pro athlete, yet he was unhappy. Junior, the life of the party and so full of enthusiasm, one night found himself ready to end it all. People who knew Junior might have said at one point that he was beyond hope and a prayer. Nevertheless, as explained in Junior Miller's story, he cried out to God for forgiveness and was saved. God is not limited in His ability to heal and forgive.

Junior was not going through some kind of emotional phase where he simply decided to do the right thing and go to church. The change came from within. He surrendered his life to the Lord and sought with all his heart to live for Him.

As a result, God blessed him in many ways. God healed his marriage; enabled him to overcome dyslexia; helped him overcome bankruptcy and start a business; but above all—God rescued his soul.

As we catch a glimpse of the miracles within Junior Miller's life, we can learn some valuable lessons.

1. Failure is never final. Junior proved that failure is never final. Yes, he did live a destructive lifestyle for many years and had to endure the consequences. However, because he sought the Lord's forgiveness whole-heartedly, his failures were not beyond God's healing touch.

The Bible puts it this way: "The one who confesses and forsakes his mistakes gets another chance" (Proverbs 28:13).

In the game of life, all of us at one time or another have taken the ball and run in the wrong direction. We all have stumbled and fumbled our way through life, but God says, "Get up and get back in the game. It isn't over yet!"

2. Never, never, never stop praying and sharing your faith with others. Throughout his successful college and pro career, it took several years for Junior Miller to discover what Solomon discovered years before. "I said to myself, 'Come now, I will test you with pleasure. So enjoy yourself.' And behold, it too was futility" (Ecclesiastes 2:1). Solomon's statement could be paraphrased, "I found no lasting value in this attempt." Junior realized the empty pursuit of self and found lasting value in a relationship with Jesus Christ. Junior expressed how many people had been praying for him over the years.

Is there anyone in your life, perhaps yourself, whom you feel is beyond God's reach? Never underestimate the power of prayer and God's saving grace.

LESSON ELEVEN

Positive Peer Pressure

"We are called to live out the gospel radically. And to do that in today's culture means getting out of our comfort zone!" stated Nebraska receivers' coach Ron Brown.

Getting out of our comfort zone means being available for God to work in our life. For former Cornhusker receiver Todd Brown, one such time in his life involved offering positive peer pressure when he was a high school student. During his prep years, he felt a sense of mission and purpose to be part of a spiritual movement amidst the small central Nebraska town of Holdrege.

"God started a revival in our town," Todd reflected. "God was using positive peer pressure. We took our Bibles to school. We confronted kids who were partying. We took our faith seriously. We took it very seriously, but we were a very light-hearted, fun-loving group. We just tried to show the world that being a Christian is absolutely, positively the best life one could ever lead."

We live in a time when society's values have been turned upside down. A generation ago, the content of today's typical movie, television program, or magazine would have been considered by society to be immoral. Some scholars argue that we have lowered our standards and are now living in a post-Christian era. In fact, many believe that humanism has reached an all-time high. False solutions are offered in every area of life. But even though these times may be difficult, the Apostle Paul offers us some advice on how to handle times like these: "Preach the Word; be prepared in season and out of season; correct, rebuke and encourage—with great patience and careful instruction. For the time will come when men will not put up with sound doctrine. Instead, to suit their own desires, they will gather around them a great number of teachers to say what their itching ears want to hear. They will turn their ears away from the truth and turn aside to myths. But you, keep your head in all situations, endure hardship, do the work of an evangelist, discharge all the duties of your ministry" (2 Timothy 4:2-5).

Todd Brown demonstrated that it is still possible to walk with God and take a stand against popular culture. Based upon Paul's advice, here is how we can be faithful in times like these:

1. Make the Bible your playbook for life. Many segments of our society have a tendency to push aside Scripture and substitute the wisdom of men and women. Whether it's to prevent drug use or teen pregnancy, many so-called experts offer their best advice, which falls far short of God's advice if it neglects the Bible. Any program, even with the best intentions, makes a terrible mistake by overlooking God's blueprint for life.

2. Be ready to respond. Every athlete understands the need for preparation. Without preparation, we can be more easily influenced by the world's standards. Paul's advice to be ready means to "be at hand, to have an alert mind." It's the idea of being ready to serve God in any situation, whether it is convenient or not. Think biblically about the important issues of our day and be sensitive to how God may want you to respond.

3. Take a stand. Sooner or later, each of us is responsible for our actions. At some point during a game, an athlete must step forward and make the shot or pass that will help determine the outcome of the game. For the Christian, taking a stand means correcting, rebuking, and encouraging—when it's appropriate. It means doing the right thing, even when others around us don't.

Todd Brown sought to honor God and reach others for Christ at his public high school. His decision was based upon God's Word as he looked for opportunities to share his faith with others. Can we do anything less in our lives?

LESSON TWELVE

Coach Finds Redemption

Kevin Steele, former Nebraska inside linebackers' coach (1989-94) and present Baylor head coach, admitted that he strayed from God some years prior to his coaching stint at Nebraska. Yet, he found forgiveness and the God-given ability to change his ways.

"I fell into the sinful ways of the world," he said.

The guilt from those deeds left him empty and miserable, but upon confessing his sin to God and asking for His forgiveness, Steele said he found hope.

"You have things that you have confessed, but you really haven't let go. And I realized that Christ died for my sins, and I don't have to leave those things hanging on my back anymore. I'm forgiven. One of my favorite verses is John 19:30 when Jesus had received the sour wine just before dying on the cross. He said, 'It is finished.' It is finished when you give your life to Christ. Start anew, talk anew, and live anew because His last words on the cross were, 'It is finished.' "

Though he had fallen into sin, Kevin Steele found redemption and reconciliation through Christ's forgiveness. This illustration brings to mind a familiar story about redemption and reconciliation—the parable of the lost son.

A handful of principles are presented in this parable. In Luke 15:11-32, Jesus explained how a young man foolishly wasted his inheritance given to him by his father in advance. Hungry and broke, the son returned home to ask his father's forgiveness. The father readily forgave and took him in without reservation. With both Coach Steele and the prodigal son, there are important lessons about life that none of us should forget.

1. Some people need to hit bottom before they come to their senses. The younger son, like many in our society, had to hit bottom before he came to his senses. "He longed to fill his stomach with the pods that the pigs were eating, but no one gave him anything. When he came to his senses, he said, 'How many of my father's hired men have food to spare, and here I am starving to death'" (Luke 15:16-17). His statement shows how far he had sunk in his life. According to Moses' law, pigs were considered unclean and were not to be eaten or used for sacrifices. For any Jew to be reduced to feeding pigs would have been a tremendous humiliation. Unfortunately, for some people it takes years before they hit bottom and come to their senses.

2. God waits patiently for us to come to our senses—we should do likewise for others, too. God's love is patient. He waits for us to respond to His love and acceptance. He doesn't treat us like robots. He gives us the opportunity to respond to Him, but He never forces us to come to Him. Like the father of the lost son, God waits patiently for us to come to our senses.

3. Be willing to forgive and accept anyone who offends you, rather than seeking revenge. The older brother couldn't forgive and forget the injustice he felt his brother had caused his family. The older brother's anger and bitterness left him just as lost as his brother. So, too, our lives can never be complete without God's patient love and forgiveness.

LESSON THIRTEEN

Quarterback Keeps Composure

Barely one minute remained in the 1984 National Championship Orange Bowl as Nebraska, trailing Miami 31-24, faced fourth and eight at the Miami 24-yard line. Consistently confident, Husker quarterback and offensive captain Turner Gill knew it was not over. He knew his team could get it done.

"In the huddle, I was reminding the players, 'When we score, don't get too excited because we are going to go for two points. When we score, don't celebrate too much because we have to get in the huddle and get ready to go for two points.' "

On the ensuing play, Gill looked for All-American receiver Irving Fryar, but opted to keep the ball. Shy of the first down marker, Gill pitched to trailing running back Jeff Smith. Smith pounded his way to the end zone for a 24-yard score.

Nebraska's bid for the national championship did fall short on the next play as a two-point conversion pass from Gill to Smith was tipped away by a Hurricane defender. Nevertheless, quarterback Gill directed the Husker offense to a down-to-the-wire finish by staying focused and keeping his composure.

On that January night in 1984, Nebraska trailed Miami nearly the entire game. The team could have given up amidst the tension of playing in the loud Orange Bowl on the Hurricanes' home field, but they didn't. Turner Gill's cool confidence throughout the contest was probably a big reason that they didn't fold. Turner exhibited two important principles that night and throughout his college football career: 1) Stay relaxed in a tense situation. 2) Do not dwell on the result if you want to win.

These principles can be found in Scripture as well:

1. Stay relaxed in a tense situation. One of the principles God teaches us through the Apostle Paul is the concept of isolation. In this concept, you isolate the past from your mind and totally concentrate on your goal. Paul was completely focused on his ultimate goal—to become conformed to the likeness of Jesus. He wrote: "Brothers, I do not consider myself yet to have taken hold of it. But one thing I do: Forgetting what is behind and straining toward what is ahead, I press on toward the goal to win the prize for which God has called me heavenward in Christ Jesus" (Philippians 3:13-14). Paul teaches us two ways to stay relaxed in any situation.

First, forget the past. The word Paul uses for "forgetting," in Philippians 3:13-14, means to completely forget. The event was no longer in his conscious mind. It's the idea of putting the event behind you. If we fail to isolate the past from the present, we run the risk of tensing up during competition. After all, who hasn't felt somewhat nervous following failure in the athletic arena? For example: If your opponent in tennis had soundly beaten you, then the natural reaction would be nervousness when you face him/her in the next match. Don't dwell on the past.

Second, Paul teaches us to pursue our goal. The word "press" actually means to pursue—to actively go after something. It's focusing all of your energy on achieving your goal. Paul's point is, by no longer thinking about the past, you can't completely leave the event behind. But by putting the event in the past, and then, by deliberately focusing your attention on the goal, you can stay relaxed. The positive action of focusing on the goal keeps the negative experience from influencing you.

Be sure to practice isolation following every event, whether it's good or bad. The attitude of disappointment or over-confidence will not be a problem if you pursue the ultimate goal of Christ-likeness. If we focus on our responsibilities, rather than the results, then we can maximize our God-given talents and abilities.

2. Do not dwell on the result if you want to win. The best way to not dwell on the result is to focus on the process or journey instead. The Bible defines winning by the effort we put forth toward our goal of Christ-likeness, rather than the result on the scoreboard. "Whatever you do, work at it with all your heart, as working for the Lord, not for men" (Colossians 3:23).

If we focus on our responsibilities rather than the results, then we can maximize our God-given talents and abilities. And we won't waste our time and energy worrying about the outcome.

LESSON FOURTEEN

Frost Ignores Boos

Husker quarterback Scott Frost had lived under a microscope since his prep All-American days at Wood River High in west central Nebraska. A transfer from Stanford, many fans had not welcomed him back to his native state with open arms. Thus, expectations mounted high upon him for his senior season. During the second game of the 1997 national championship campaign, some fans booed him during a 38-24 win over Central Florida in Lincoln. A week later, he would travel to Seattle to play then No. 2 Washington at Husky Stadium, an arena regarded as one of the loudest in college football.

"At that point I felt there was a lot of burden on my shoulders," Frost recalled, "because there wasn't really anyone behind me, including a lot of my own fans. It was a tough time on me. It was a time when I could've given up, I could've been down on myself."

Nevertheless, Frost laid those feelings aside and focused on executing to the best of his ability. During the matchup, Frost exploded with two rushing touchdowns in the first quarter to set the game's tone, as No. 7 Nebraska charged to a 27-14 upset. Frost's 97 yards on the ground, 88 through the air, and two rushing touchdowns led to his being named the ABC-TV Chevrolet Player of the Game.

"I think you just get stronger with experience through the ups and the downs," Frost said later, regarding the pressure he had felt. "Getting through them just makes you stronger and more able to respond to things better."

Persistent—the word is a fitting description of Scott Frost. Here are several thoughts on persistence and determination:

"Nothing in the world can take the place of persistence. Talent will not; nothing is more common than unsuccessful men with talent. Genius will not; unrewarded genius is almost a proverb. Education will not; the world is full of educated derelicts. Persistence and determination alone are omnipotent." —Calvin Coolidge

"Many people fail in life because they believe in the adage 'If you don't succeed, try something else.' But success eludes those who follow such advice. Virtually everyone has had dreams at one time or another, especially in youth. The dreams that have come true did so because people stuck to their ambitions. They refused to be discouraged. They never let disappointment get the upper hand. Challenges only spurred them on to greater effort." —Don Owens

"When Jesus tells us to 'seek first the kingdom of God,' the very word 'seek' implies a strong-minded pursuit. *J.B. Phillips* paraphrases the idea with 'set your heart on.' *The Amplified Bible* says, 'Aim at and strive after.' The Greek text of Matthew's Gospel states a continual command: 'Keep on continually seeking . . .' The thought is determination, which I define as 'deciding to hang tough, regardless.' " —Charles Swindoll

Persistence and determination are two important

character qualities needed by every Christian. You see, the spiritual life of a Christian is much more like a cross-country run than a sprint. And those who don't fizzle out at the end of the race are people who don't get discouraged. If you want to know someone's character, examine how they respond to adversity. How one deals with criticism and failure often reveals more about a person's character than his success. How do you respond when things don't go your way? When someone unjustly criticizes you? When you fall short of your expectations? When everything seems to go against you?

As a Christian, you don't need to gut it out on your own. It's a matter of relying on God for your strength. God can do amazing things through us, by His power. Jesus said, "Apart from me you can do nothing" (John 15:5). The Apostle Paul said, "Now to Him who is able to do immeasurably more than all we ask or imagine, according to His power that is at work within us" (Ephesians 3:20).

Remember, when you are faced with an impossible situation, stretch out your courage, hang tough, and depend on Him. The Bible says, "Let us not get tired of doing what is right, for after a while we will reap a harvest of blessing if we don't get discouraged and give up" (Galatians 6:9). Allow God to help you through difficult times. He alone provides the power and the strength to enable us to consistently serve Him each day of our lives. "I can do all things through Christ who gives me the strength" (Philippians 4:13).

LESSON FIFTEEN

A Gracious Competitor

Gracious and competitive are not synonymous terms, but they blend well in describing the character of former Nebraska walk-on quarterback Travis Turner. Turner, a 6-foot-3 signal caller from Scottsbluff, Neb., spent his final two seasons battling for and losing the starting job.

During the 1984 season, Turner and senior Craig Sundberg split time at the signal caller spot. Following a frustrating 17-7 loss to Oklahoma that derailed then No. 1 Nebraska's shot at a national championship, Turner found himself as the number-two guy going into the bowl game.

"Craig won back the starting job after the Oklahoma game," Turner noted. "He started the Sugar Bowl and won the MVP, and I was grateful to be a part of it. It was a difficult year for Craig, and God really honored his faithfulness."

Several months later, Travis Turner was the senior quarterback, again battling for the starting nod. But a back injury and a torn anterior-cruciate ligament hampered him the remainder of his career. His inability to practice deterred his performance as McCathorn Clayton took over the reins. And though frustrated by his decline, Turner opted to make the most of an opportunity.

"I really struggled, but God taught me a lot through it. I specifically remember the Lord convicting me to pray for him [Clayton]. That really became my focus. I was just praying for Mac and wanting God to bless him, and it softened my heart. I just did my best to encourage and be supportive.

"One of the biggest things I learned was that God's vision and purpose for our lives is a lot bigger than ours. He's not wrapped up in worldly success. He's truly interested in building our character. And if we can find that in our circumstances, then we can grow. But if we're constantly looking at the circumstances or the score, then we are going to miss out on His blessings."

Through learning that truth, Travis Turner became a gracious competitor.

It's not easy to love someone you're competing with, especially if you believe you aren't being treated fairly. But God commands us to love unconditionally. He doesn't call us to be wimps, but to be more like Christ. And while Travis Turner didn't consider any of his teammates as enemies, the Bible instructs us to love even those who do nothing to deserve it.

"But I tell you: Love your enemies and pray for those who persecute you, that you may be sons of your Father in heaven. He causes His sun to rise on the evil and the good and sends rain on the righteous and the unrighteous. If you love those who love you, what reward will you get? Are not even the tax collectors doing that? And if you greet only your brothers, what are you doing more than others? Do not even pagans do that? Be perfect, therefore, as your heavenly Father is perfect" (Matthew 5:44-48).

Jesus directed His remarks toward a group of religious teachers known as the Scribes and Pharisees, who were proud, prejudiced, judgmental, and vengeful men who acted with holier-than-thou attitudes. For this group of men, Jesus' teaching must have seemed crazy. After all, these so-called spiritual leaders not only felt they had the right to hate their enemies, but also the duty to hate their enemies.

Jesus exposed this perverted teaching by commanding the religious teachers to love their enemies. The concept of loving your personal enemy wasn't even new—the Old Testament taught it, but the religious teachers had ignored God's truth. The problem the religious teachers had with Jesus' teaching is not much different than our problem today with loving our enemies. All of us tend to base love on the desirability of the object of our love. We love attractive people, fun recreation, enjoyable hobbies, and impressive possessions. But God's love is unconditional and self-sacrificing. When the Good Samaritan sacrificed his own convenience, resources, and safety to meet another's needs, he demonstrated true love.

The Bible uses four different terms for the word "love." The love Jesus is talking about here is "agape," the love that seeks and works to meet another's highest good. This type of love might involve emotion, but it always involves action. A great example of this is Paul's teaching on love in 1 Corinthians 13, where all 15 characteristics of love are given in verb form.

Don't retaliate when someone attacks you. Instead, by loving and praying for your enemies, you can overcome evil with good. No one demonstrated this more than Jesus Himself. Can you imagine the pain of betrayal Jesus must have felt when He was unjustly put to death on the cross? Most of us will never know the anxiety and stress that Jesus experienced the last days of His life. But His example of overcoming evil with love should inspire us to do likewise. After all, each one of us was His enemy until we became one of His followers.

Travis Turner understood how God desires for us to be more like Christ. He prayed for and encouraged his rival teammates. And it's only by our submission to the Lord that He can truly enable us to love others.

LESSON SIXTEEN

Berringer Handles Backup Role

During the majority of his quarterback career with the Huskers, the late Brook Berringer spent his time as a backup to 1995 All-American Tommie Frazier, but he chose not to let it bother him. Brook's opportunity to start came during Nebraska's '94 championship run when Frazier was sidelined with a blood clot behind his right knee. Brook started and won seven games. But in 1995 with Frazier healthy, the tall signal caller from Goodland, Kan., found himself again on the sideline. And though Berringer possessed the ability to start almost anywhere else in the country, he never publicly complained about it. He was a team player.

"He handled a tough situation as well as and with about as much dignity as anybody ever could, in terms of his playing situation," Coach Tom Osborne said.

For Brook, his source of inner strength and contentment was his faith in Jesus Christ.

"When I have something more specific to focus on, like eternal life, my faith and Christianity, and my yearning just to grow in that faith, it brings everything—the whole scheme of things into focus," he said. "It's just amazing, the difference that it's made in my life. I know where I'm headed, the ultimate goal, and it brings everything into perspective. It makes football, although it is a big part of my life, something that is not as important as maybe I once thought. And it really prioritizes things in my life."

An old Greek motto says: You will break the bow if you keep it always bent.

Stress is caused by two opposing forces that pull against each other. Whether it's the force of a bow being bent or the pressure of unhappy fans, stress adds undue pressure to our lives. Sometimes stress is created by the demands others place on us. Their "shoulds" and "musts" hit us like a linebacker sacking a quarterback.

Stress can be overcome, as Berringer discovered, by using God's strategy to defeat worry. Check out Proverbs 3:5-6. Notice where it's our responsibility to tackle worry and where it's God's responsibility to tackle worry.

"Trust [my part] in the Lord with all your heart, and do not lean [my part] on your own understanding. In all your ways acknowledge [my part] Him, and He will make your paths straight [God's part]" (Proverbs 3:5-6).

It's important to understand several of these key terms in Proverbs. Here is a breakdown of their meaning, using football as an illustration:

1. Trust. When a receiver runs a pass route, the quarterback places his trust in his receiver to run the correct play. If his receiver turns the wrong way or stops short on his pass pattern, the quarterback's throw is off the mark. The idea of trust in this verse is throwing oneself down and lying extended on the ground, casting all hopes for the present and the future on another. We are to place our complete trust in the Lord with all of our heart. How many times have you heard someone refer to a player who competes with a lot of heart? When NFL television commentator John Madden refers to a football player with heart, he doesn't mean the organ in the chest that pumps blood. He's talking about the same thing the Bible refers to as one's "inner person," that part of us which represents our emotion, intellect, and will. It's the idea of not holding anything back.

2. Do not lean. This is a negative command. The best comparison may be a defensive lineman who is warned not to lean into the neutral zone, otherwise he is likely to be flagged for being offside. The idea in this verse is don't lean on your own ingenuity to work out your problems. In college football, it's oftentimes the freshmen who make mental mistakes. In the NFL, it's rookies who, for lack of understanding, blow it. It's often because they try to work things out on their own, rather than asking for advice or spending time in their playbook. This verse in Proverbs is a warning about relying too much on human understanding, rather than on God's wisdom.

Next, we'll look at the last two terms and how you can manage your stress. Remember to completely trust in God and don't place your understanding of a stressful situation on yourself.

LESSON SEVENTEEN

Husker Offense
Confident in the Clutch

Many adjectives could be used to describe the 1997 national championship Cornhuskers, but one moment defined the team's determination to win. It was the "miracle catch" by Nebraska freshman split end Matt Davison at Missouri. Trailing 38-31 with 1:02 left in the fourth quarter, the No. 1 Huskers took over possession at their own 33-yard line for a last chance effort. Senior quarterback Scott Frost piloted Nebraska's offense down field, managing the clock with screen passes and by spiking the ball after the snap.

Seven seconds remained with third down from the Missouri 12-yard line. Frost, looking for a receiver, fired to Shevin Wiggins at the goal line. Wiggins, hit by a defender from behind as the ball simultaneously hit him in the chest, struggled to reel it in. Juggling the ball, Wiggins fell backwards. The pigskin flew loose and bounced backwards off his foot into the empty night sky. A Tiger defender strained futilely for the loose ball. Freshman split end Matt Davison dived horizontally for the spinning oblong object. Feeling the grass between his fingers, the Tecumseh, Neb., native garnered the prize before it could touch the ground. The completion was ruled a touchdown, and the Huskers went on to win the dogfight 45-38 in overtime.

Nebraska struggled against its unranked opponent. Nevertheless, they looked past the pressure and fear of losing. They did not lose heart.

Charles H. Mayo had this to say about worry and stress: "Worry affects circulation, the heart, the glands, and the whole nervous system. I have never known a man who died from overwork, but many who died from doubt."

Sports has plenty of stressful moments, as the 1997 Cornhuskers discovered at Missouri. When competition requires two sides to push and pull against each other, there will be some stress. Although coaches probably feel the greatest amount of stress, no athlete is immune to it. In 1961, Yankee slugger Roger Maris actually lost clumps of his hair from the stress he felt on his way to breaking Babe Ruth's single-season home run record.

Let's continue to look at God's remedy for stress found in Proverbs 3:5-6.

3. Acknowledge. In this verse, acknowledge literally means to "recognize" God's presence and control. It's the idea of turning every area of life over to God. Jesus put it this way: "But seek first His kingdom and His righteousness, and all these things will be given to you as well" (Matthew 6:33). Have you acknowledged or recognized God in every area of your life? Don't leave God out of any decision you make.

4. Make Straight. Few collegiate offensive lines have received more attention than the '94 and '95 Nebraska Cornhuskers. Nicknamed the "pipeline," they opened huge holes against the defense. No one was more appreciative of their efforts than the offensive backfield. In many cases, all the ball carriers needed to do was run straight through the path that their 300-pound blockers opened.

When Proverbs refers to "make straight," it's the

thought of making something smooth, straight, or right. It's the idea of removing obstacles that are in the way. You can depend on the Lord to clear the way and smooth out your path.

God's program for stress relief involves pausing to pray. Take a step back from your circumstance and realize that God is ready to help you. God says, "Be quiet and still, and know that I am God" (Psalm 46:10 NCV). Then pray and tell God how you feel. "I pour out my problems to Him; I tell Him my troubles. When I am afraid, you, Lord, know the way out" (Psalm 142:2-3 NCV).

In good times and bad, bring your decision or circumstance to God. Look to the Bible as your playbook, and then follow God's coaching. The Master Coach will make your paths straight by both guiding and protecting you.

LESSON EIGHTEEN

Irving Fryar: Transformed by God

Former Husker All-American and NFL star wide receiver Irving Fryar was born between his sisters Faith and Hope amidst gang violence in the suburbs of southwest New Jersey. He ignored the instruction of his Christian mother and lived the neighborhood code.

"As I became a teenager, I started trying to become my own person. I was trying to figure out my own identity. I was in a gang. We robbed and we stole and we fought and we did drugs and drank and all the things that a gang does. We fought against other gangs in other towns. Every now and then someone would bring out a knife or a baseball bat or something like that."

And though Irving abandoned the gangs to attend the University of Nebraska on a football scholarship through the early 1980s, the strife remained in his heart. But in 1989, amidst his successful NFL career and his fast off-field lifestyle with drugs and other problems, Irving wanted to change and repented before God.

"The Lord was tugging at my heart. I finally got enough courage to say, 'God, I know I messed up. If You can find it in Your heart to forgive me, have Your way with me. I'll do anything you want.' And before I could even finish that prayer, God saved me. He changed my life."

The turnaround in Irving Fryar was dramatic. Formerly a violent gang member, Irving now serves boldly as an ordained minister.

Whether as a gang member in his youth or during his adult life, Irving Fryar lived as a rebel until he repented before God. Ultimately, he found his self-serving lifestyle led to emptiness. Similarly, we live in a world where, sadly, more and more people believe freedom means to do whatever they want. Yet, that kind of freedom is ultimately slavery to sin as mankind becomes controlled by his desires and lusts. True freedom comes with a price tag called responsibility. However, that price, when paid, is ultimately liberating.

Imagine comparing the cost of freedom to one who is navigating a large ship in the middle of the ocean. In order to reach the destination, the pilot can't simply travel any which way he wishes. He must follow a specific course to avoid getting lost. He must literally enslave himself to his compass and navigational instruments to have the freedom of the seas. Only a fool would choose to act defiantly toward his navigational instruments. Yet, that's how many people respond toward God's direction in the Bible. Sadly, many people choose to ignore or discredit God's biblical truth. The Bible predicted that these acts of rebellion and stubbornness would happen "in the last days" (2 Timothy 3:1-2).

How does God view defiance? In the Bible, we read about King Saul who did his own thing, just as much as Irving Fryar once did his own thing. God had provided instruction through the prophet-judge Samuel, but Saul chose to defy God's will. When Samuel confronted Saul about his defiance toward God, he told him, "For rebellion is as bad as the sin of witchcraft, and stubbornness is as bad as worshipping idols" (1 Samuel

15:23a, TLB). It's pretty obvious from this analogy that God doesn't think too much of a stubborn or rebellious attitude.

It's not only the unbeliever that struggles with defiance, but also believers. And it's not something that happens suddenly. Another Old Testament example of compromise and defiance is seen in the life of King Solomon. The progression of defiance seems to follow the same pattern of compromise, followed by wild living and an unwillingness to be accountable to anyone else. Solomon defied God by marrying a lot of foreign women who turned his heart away from God for a period of time.

What happens when we choose to defy God? Here is a statement made by Lord Byron many years ago that still applies today: "The thorns which I have reap'd are of the tree I planted; they have torn me, and I bleed. I should have known what fruit would spring from such a seed." God uses the thorns that grow from our life to prick us back on the right path. Since He misses the close fellowship He had with us and wishes to regain it, He may discipline us. To defy God is to guarantee a miserable life. "The way of the treacherous is hard" (Proverbs 13:15b).

A coach I know chose to defy God by becoming involved in an immoral relationship. This coach's excuse was, "That's just the way I am. God made me this way."

We should never forget that there are consequences for our actions. And we should be careful not to rationalize our behavior, otherwise we can count on God taking action toward our defiance. That's a gamble none of us should take.

We need to daily seek God's direction and cleansing

in our life as set forth in Psalm 139:23-24: "Search me, O God, and know my heart; test me and know my anxious thoughts. See if there is any offensive way in me and lead me in the way everlasting."

LESSON NINETEEN

Player Remembers the Cross

The most hostile battles in football are often fought on the front lines. And for former All-American center Aaron Graham of Nebraska's 1994 and 1995 national championship teams, those intense on-field collisions have proven to be character revealing.

"Sometimes it's rough," said the 6-foot-4, 285-pound interior lineman. "But I draw a symbol of the cross on my wrist tape, and that gives me a chance every play to look down at the hand that I snap the ball with and really remind myself who I'm playing for out on that field. It really helps me to stay focused in times where I might let my mouth slip. It keeps me focused on whom I'm playing for."

Before competing on the offensive line, Aaron Graham said he would remind himself of whom he needed to honor while on the field—that person being Jesus Christ, who died for him on the cross. As the center drew a symbol of the cross on his tape, he was preparing his mind for battle against foul language and unsportsman-like conduct. In a similar way, Christians are in the midst of an unseen spiritual battle and need to ready themselves with God's armor.

"Finally, be strong in the Lord and His mighty power. Put on the full armor of God so that you can take your stand against the devil's schemes. For our struggle is not against flesh and blood, but against the rulers, against the authorities, against the powers of this dark world and against the spiritual forces of evil in the heavenly realms" (Ephesians 6:10-12).

Many Christians are unaware that there is a spiritual battle going on. While they worry about who will win the big games or how their favorite player will perform, they fail to realize that there's a spiritual contest going on with life-and-death consequences.

What would be the chance for a batter to get a hit against a major league pitcher if he were wearing a blindfold? It wouldn't be good. Nor does it make any sense to be unaware of Satan's strategies. This spiritual contest may be invisible, but both sides are playing for keeps.

Any team preparing for a game must first study its opponent. How well do you know the enemy? Here is a brief scouting report: First, Satan is an angel who was thrown out of heaven because he rebelled against God's authority (Isaiah 14:12-14). Second, he wants to not only beat you, but wipe you out. "Your enemy the devil prowls around like a roaring lion looking for someone to devour" (1 Peter 5:8). Finally, Satan met his match in the person of Jesus Christ. "Since the children have flesh and blood, He too shared in their humanity so that by His death He might destroy him who holds the power of death—that is, the devil—and free those who all their lives were held in slavery by their fear of death" (Hebrews 2:14-15).

A few years ago, NFL running back Thurman Thomas couldn't locate his football helmet during a game. There was a lot of confusion and scrambling as everyone tried to find it. Equipment doesn't do us much good unless we wear it. Are you wearing the equipment that God has provided?

According to Ephesians 6:13-17, we should put on our spiritual armor each day:

- "The belt of truth"—Be honest and faithful. Keep your commitments.
- "The breastplate of righteousness"—Live a godly and righteous life.
- "Feet fitted with...the gospel of peace"—Share the gospel with others.
- "The shield of faith"—Trust God for your security and strength against Satan.
- "The helmet of salvation"—This provides confidence for the battle.
- "The sword of the Spirit, which is the word of God"— Our only offensive weapon. Use it!

We face a powerful team of demonic forces whose goal is to defeat the church. We need to rely on God's armor and direction to obtain the victory!

LESSON TWENTY

Quarterback Recovers From Leg Injury

August two-a-days, to prepare for the 1982 college football season, were on the horizon when Husker junior quarterback Turner Gill sported a unique T-shirt for media day. On the previous New Year's Day, the Cornhuskers had lost the national championship by a touchdown to Clemson in the Orange Bowl and were hungry for a national title. Many felt that Turner Gill's ability and leadership would be key to making that happen.

On Nov. 14, 1981, Gill suffered nerve damage in his lower right leg at home against Iowa State. The injury sidelined him for the remainder of his sensational sophomore season. Gill endured two surgeries and a lengthy rehabilitation process before experiencing any more physical contact. By fall, he received the okay for full contact.

Thus on that August media day, his shirt bore a simple message to clear up any questions as to his future playing status. It read, "The leg's ok. I'm gonna play. Are there any more [questions]?"

NU fans' hopes were confirmed. The returning All-Big Eight quarterback was back and ready.

For Christians, there should be a heartfelt eagerness about the return of Jesus Christ, far more than there is for the superstar athletes we watch. With former Nebraska quarterback Turner Gill in 1982, fans could only hope that his leg would be recovered so he could be given medical clearance to play. But for Christians, we know for a fact that Jesus Christ will return.

"Look, He is coming with the clouds, and every eye will see Him, even those who pierced Him; and all the peoples of the earth will mourn because of Him. So shall it be! Amen" (Revelation 1:7).

John's words in the book of Revelation read like a press release. He is announcing the return of Jesus to earth. Talk about good ratings! Everyone will see Him arrive, and they will know it is Jesus. And while we may eagerly await the amazing athletic feats by a sidelined star athlete, nothing compares to what Jesus will accomplish when He conquers evil and judges all people according to their deeds (Mark 20:11-15).

The return of Christ is often referred to as "The Second Coming," and it's no minor issue in the Bible. God's Word mentions the return of Christ or the end of time every 30 verses. Only four of 27 New Testament books do not mention Christ's return.

While Gill's return was determined by his health, Christ's return is certain. But we don't know when it will be. The Bible says, "Now brothers, about times and dates we do not need to write you, for you know very well that the day of the Lord will come like a thief in the night" (1 Thessalonians 5:1-2).

No one can accurately predict the date of Christ's return, so it's foolish to try and pinpoint the exact day. While Christians often disagree about what events will lead up to the return of Christ, there is little disagreement about what will happen once Christ does return:

1. Christ will return visibly with a loud command.

2. There will be a clear and understandable cry from an angel.
3. There will be a trumpet fanfare that is unequaled in history.
4. Believers in Christ who are dead will rise from the grave.
5. Believers in Christ who are alive will be caught up in the clouds to meet Jesus.

Since the time of the Lord's return will be unexpected, we should always be ready for His coming. Suppose He were to return today. How would He find you living? Are you ready for His return? Shouldn't we live each day as if Christ were going to come back at any time?

LESSON TWENTY-ONE

Deaf Player Refuses Label

November 3, 1990, marked senior day at Memorial Stadium in Lincoln. A cold, light rain fell as 76,000 fans stood and raised their arms to honor Nebraska senior Kenny Walker with a deaf applause. The hulking defensive tackle jogged onto the field and raised his right arm to the masses, signing the words, "I love you" in gratitude and genuine affection.

Though Kenny could not hear the roar of the crowd, he could feel their appreciation in his heart. The road had not been easy for him. Walker had lost complete hearing at age two following a coma, but he spent his life refusing to accept the label "handicapped" regarding his disability. Kenny looked for ways to adapt amidst a world of sounds. During his senior season at Nebraska, he earned All-American status on the field and academic all-conference in the classroom. In 1991, the Denver Broncos drafted him in the eighth round, thus he spent two NFL seasons playing in the Mile-High City. Kenny Walker has truly been an overcomer.

Everyone has a weakness. Kenny Walker has obviously been at somewhat of a physical disadvantage, as he can't hear. Nevertheless, he has not let it stop him from living life to the fullest. He has battled to not allow it to handicap him. He did not want it to be an Achilles' heel.

What is an "Achilles' heel"? If you remember your Greek mythology, Achilles was the son of Peleus, King of the Myrmidons, and Thetis, a sea goddess. Achilles was considered the bravest and most handsome warrior in the army. During his childhood, he was dipped into the magical waters of the river Styx. Every part of his body that touched the water became invulnerable. Only his heel was untouched by the water. Thus, we get the term "Achilles' heel."

Each of us has our own Achilles' heel. For some, it's pride; for others, money. For Samson, it was sensuality. He's the Bible's Superman. He killed a lion with his bare hands and later beat a thousand-man army with only the jawbone of a donkey. But even Superman is vulnerable to something. For him it was kryptonite; for Samson it was his lustful desire for women.

While Kenny's physical limitation is obvious, many of us are like Samson when it comes to vulnerability in our relationship with God—we have a blind spot. What is your Achilles' heel? Is it anger . . . worry . . . greed . . . alcohol . . . drugs . . . your friends . . . selfishness . . . lust . . . pride? Here are a few lessons from the life of Samson (see Judges 13-15):

1. Surround yourself with friends that will help you identify any blind spots in your life. "Faithful are the wounds of a friend, but deceitful are the kisses of an enemy" (Proverbs 27:6). A true friend has your best interests at heart and will give you advice that is for your own good. An enemy, by contrast, may say nice things that you want to hear, but may ruin your life.

2. Know the source of your strength. Samson didn't see God as the real source of his strength. Instead, he saw only his own strength (see Judges 15:14-17). God allowed Samson's strength to be taken away so he would learn that he was weak without God's power. Don't become dependent upon your own talents and abilities. Otherwise, you may find God teaching you a painful lesson about leaning on Him, rather than yourself. Do you depend on God for your security, strength, and safety?

3. God can help you overcome past defeats. Even though God had disciplined Samson for blowing it, God still came to his aid when he reached out. Samson said, "O Lord God, please remember me . . ." (Judges 16:28). Although you may feel like God has forgotten you, He never forgets you. In spite of Samson's past failure, God still answered his prayer and destroyed the pagan temple.

Don't let your Achilles' heel defeat you. Instead of being fearful or blindsided by your weakness, let God provide the power to help you reach your potential.

LESSON TWENTY-TWO

Great Teams Find Strength in Bonding

Clester Johnson, a former NU wingback from the 1994 and 1995 championship teams, said that team unity was lacking in his early years as a Husker.

"When I first got here, there wasn't much unity on the football team," he recalled. "The year before [1990] they got plastered by [unranked] Oklahoma 45-10 and got beat by [eventual United Press International National Champion] Georgia Tech 45-21 in the Citrus Bowl. We wanted to win bowl games. We got tired of hearing that we couldn't win the big one.

"I think the more unified we got, the better the team got. Coach Osborne implemented a unity council and discussed how we talked to each other. He also talked about what we do off the field that distracts us from doing better on the field. We needed to encourage each other more and keep each other out of difficult situations. So, collectively, we had more guys wanting to move in a better direction."

Unified, the Huskers nearly upset eventual national champion Florida State in the Jan. 1, 1994, Orange Bowl. And within two years, they had earned back-to-back titles. They had discovered the value of team unity.

Team awards can be much more rewarding than chasing individual glory. It's a matter of putting the emphasis on the team, rather than the individual. Most coaches believe that a team can't reach its potential without putting the emphasis on team unity, rather than a few individuals. The Bible also has a lot to say about teamwork, rather than self-promotion. An acrostic for the word "team" spans the next several chapters. It illustrates key characteristics of teamwork.

Time together. You can't develop relationships between the members of the team unless they spend time together. You can see the problem each year in the NBA when they play the All-Star game. Throwing together the best players in the league doesn't necessarily guarantee the best team performances. Since their practice time is limited, you rarely see the kind of teamwork that is part of the regular season. Many of the greatest teams in sports history have been veteran teams like the Steelers in football, the Celtics in basketball, and the Yankees in baseball.

Jesus spent three years with His disciples. Their cohesiveness and team spirit wouldn't have been possible without the time they spent together. The result of their teamwork impacted history. No team has ever had a greater impact on the world than Jesus Christ and His disciples. Time together is part of what makes a team successful. But it's also what you do during that time that brings a team together. Here are a couple of important characteristics of successful teams:

Trust. Trust is the emotional glue that holds a team together. When you can depend upon your teammates to do their part, then you can put all your energies into your job. Mistrust causes others to slow down or move cautiously through their task. The only way to build trust among teammates is to act consistently. The early church had to trust one another as it began to expand its influence. "Paul and Barnabas appointed elders for them in each church and with prayer and fasting committed them to the Lord, in whom they had put their trust" (Acts 14:23).

Patience. Every member of a team needs patience. Sometimes it's needed by the players who sit on the bench. Other times it's the more experienced members of the team who need to be patient with the less experienced members as they learn the system. And always there is the need to listen patiently to the coach or other teammates as they share their ideas. When we talk too much and listen too little, we communicate to others that we don't think too much of their ideas. "Everyone should be quick to listen, slow to speak and slow to become angry" (James 1:19).

Love. The Bible often talks about a love that is very different from what many call love in our society. Real love is not lust. Unlike lust, God's kind of love is directed outward toward others, not inward toward ourselves—it's unselfish! And most importantly, God's kind of love is not based upon conditions. Fans love teams and athletes—if they win. But if they hit a losing streak— forget it. That kind of love is based upon a set of conditions. God's love is unconditional. During the Jan. 1, 1995, Orange Bowl, Nebraska's All-American offensive guard Zach Wiegert told his teammates that regardless of the outcome of the game, he would still love them. That's unconditional love. The Apostle Paul defines love in 1 Corinthians chapter 13, and then he encourages us to just do it in chapter 14.

LESSON TWENTY-THREE

Offensive Lineman Encourages Teammates

Former Nebraska All-American offensive lineman and NFL veteran Bob Newton recalled the teamwork needed to beat Louisiana State for a share of the 1970 national title. Trailing 12-10 in the fourth quarter, the Huskers faced perhaps the best defensive team in the country. But Nebraska's offense responded confidently with a nearly eight-minute, 14-play touchdown drive. The series was emotionally draining and exhilarating and was extremely physically demanding, Newton described.

"I loved it," he said. "When I was in the huddle, I would try to communicate confidence to the other linemen and to [quarterback] Jerry [Tagge] and [I-back] Jeff [Kinney]. I wanted that backfield to feel confident that the holes were going to be there—that we would open them up for them, and also that Jerry would have time to pass the ball. As an offensive lineman, I always tried to exude confidence to my teammates."

Thus, with 6:10 remaining and the end zone a yard away, quarterback Tagge kept the ball and dived over the middle of the pile. He stretched across the goal line for the eventual winning score as Nebraska led 17-12.

The 1970 Cornhusker football team, as talented as it was, never lost sight of the importance of teamwork. And a key member of Nebraska's offensive front line, Bob Newton, knew the value of encouraging that unity for the team to reach its potential.

Previously we examined the first part of our **T-E-A-M** acrostic: Time spent together. As we continue our look at teamwork, here are the next two characteristics:

Encourage your teammates. The Apostle Paul knew how important it was not only to be encouraged by his teammates, but also to be an encouragement to them. "Paul sent for the disciples, and after encouraging them, said good-bye and set out for Macedonia. He traveled through that area, speaking many words of encouragement to the people . . ." (Acts 20:1, 2). While you may not have as much talent to offer your team, encouragement is something everyone can offer. We all need to be encouragers. Paul said, "Therefore encourage one another and build each other up" (1 Thessalonians 5:11).

What you say to a teammate does affect his/her attitude. And if you affect his/her attitude, you've potentially affected the behavior of the entire team. If the Apostle Paul were your coach, here is what he might say: "Do not let any unwholesome talk come out of your mouths, but only what is helpful for building others up according to their needs, that it may benefit those who listen" (Ephesians 4:29). There is little doubt that positive feedback builds up and improves athletic performance. That's why most teams prefer to play at home. When 76,000 screaming fans are yelling, "Go for it!" it's pretty hard to give less than your best effort.

Here are a few suggestions on how to encourage your teammates:

A word of encouragement. Call out their names if they make a good play. If they blow it, reassure them that it's only temporary. Be as specific and natural as you can. You don't need to flatter them—just be honest. Let your teammates know that you appreciate them. "Oil and perfume make the heart glad, so a man's counsel is sweet to his friend" (Proverbs 27:9).

High-five, hug, or handshake. Any appropriate physical acknowledgment will be appreciated.

A warm smile. Don't fake it! Be yourself, but don't walk around with a frown on your face. "When a king's face brightens, it means life; his favor is like a rain cloud in spring" (Proverbs 16:15).

Assist your teammates. There are at least two ways you can assist your teammates:

Play your role on the team. When the ministry of Jesus was becoming more popular than that of John the Baptist, rather than being jealous of Jesus, John said, "He must become greater; I must become less" (John 3:30). John understood his role was to support Jesus by helping prepare the way for Jesus' ministry.

Look out for the best interests of your teammates. Since selfish ambition, vain conceit, and self-centeredness tear down team unity, looking out for your teammates' interests brings unity. The unselfish athlete doesn't use words like "I," "me," and "mine." Humility is what makes this possible. "In humility, consider others better than yourself. Each of you should look not only to your own interests, but also to the interests of others" (Philippians 2:3,4).

No-Name
Athlete Makes Impact

Back-up players and those who devote their allotted collegiate football careers to a minimal amount of playing time on special teams often compete with an extra amount of heart. One such athlete was David Seizys. During the early 1990s, Seizys contributed on the kickoff team and held for PATs and field goals. His role wasn't glamorous, but it was an opportunity to contribute. And he took pride in it.

"God had given me another glorious position that nobody realizes is so important until the team loses by one point," Seizys said of his job as kickholder. "It's not something that gets attention in the papers. But that's what I like because I can glorify God through the blue collar work that He has given me."

During the 1993 campaign, the senior played a key role in two pivotal moments of the season. He recovered a fumble during a kickoff against Oklahoma that led to a victory-clinching touchdown to preserve an undefeated season. And he later held for kicker Byron Bennett in a field goal attempt that would have clinched the 1993 national title from Florida State. During both plays, Seizys executed his responsibilities correctly. Though he wasn't a star, much less a starter, he knew that he was expected to perform his job with wholehearted commitment and precision. He was a team player.

In the last two devotions, we examined the first part of our **T-E-A-M** acrostic: **T** - Time spent together; **E** - Encourage your teammates; and **A** - Assist your teammates. As we continue our look at teamwork, here is our final look at the characteristics:

Maintain Team Spirit. When David Seizys ran onto the field, he emerged with vigor. He was proud to accept the responsibilities of his role on the team. He did not play with jealousy. So how can a team maintain team spirit? It begins with each of the members of team following a couple of basic fundamentals of teamwork:

Respect for your coach (leader). Respect for authority is critical to team spirit. Without a chain-of-command concept of authority, there is confusion and chaos. The chain of command is a biblical concept that God gives us so we can function properly. For team sports, the chain of command is the head coach followed by the assistant coaches and then the players.

In the New Testament, Peter writes, "Servants, be submissive to your masters with all respect . . . for this finds favor with God" (1 Peter 2:18-20). It may be difficult to respect a coach or leader who doesn't appear to deserve your respect, but you are responsible to follow their lead. Your attitude toward him or her will greatly impact how your team works together.

Forgive and forget your teammates' mistakes. Everybody blows it sooner or later. Even the most talented athletes are prone to mistakes. If you have any doubts, take a look at the NFL blooper films. These films show professional athletes who run the wrong way, drop simple passes, and fall on their faces. If a pro athlete can make mistakes, so can your teammates. "Let all bitterness and wrath and anger and clamor and slander be put away from you, along with all malice. And be kind to one another, tender-hearted, forgiving each other, just as God in Christ has forgiven you" (Ephesians 4:31-32).

In addition to forgiving, it's also important to forget. Don't fume about a teammate's mistake. The Bible says, "'Lord, how many times shall I forgive my brother when he sins against me? Up to seven times?' Jesus answered, 'I tell you not seven times, but up to seventy times seven'" (Matthew 18:21-22).

Forgetting means: 1) refusing to keep track of their mistakes; 2) not keeping score (1 Corinthians 13:5); 3) being bigger than the offense (Psalm 119:165); and 4) refusing to hold onto any judgmental attitude (Matthew 7:1-5).

The power of teamwork can improve any team's performance. A team of athletes working together can accomplish much more than the separate members working individually. That's what "synergy" is. The word synergy means, "the sum total is greater than the total of separate parts." It's the idea of working together. Some experts have estimated that if you could get all the muscles in your body to pull in one direction, you could lift over 25 tons. In Buckminster Fuller's book, *Synergetics*, he says, "One plus one can equal four if we put our efforts together in the same direction." Commit yourself to making your efforts equal more by pulling in the same direction as the rest of the team.

LESSON TWENTY-FIVE

A 'Terrible and Great Year'

Football coach Tom Osborne's range of emotions about winning a consecutive national championship was as complete as his 1995 team's 62-24 Fiesta Bowl victory over Florida.

During a short span of months, a small handful of Nebraska football players had been charged with differing individual crimes. As the truth in the various scenarios unfolded before him, he attempted to handle each with integrity. Amidst the crises there was controversy, and some in the national media charged that he was a win-at-all-costs coach.

"It was a terrible year and it was a great year," he told a press conference. "It was taxing. It was gratifying to work with a group of players with that focus and drive. And that is the saving, redeeming factor."

Osborne called that corps of players his best team ever. But the Huskers' 1995 season, despite a 25-game winning streak and back-to-back national titles, was surrounded by controversy.

So much in sports depends on your vantage point. As Coach Osborne faced a season filled with adversity and success, his perspective helped to determine his attitude.

Perspective is how we view something. The term suggests the idea of "looking through . . . seeing clearly." Like many people in America, I watched the Fiesta Bowl match-up between Nebraska and Florida. But my perspective was different from most fans—I was on the sideline taking photographs. As I took pictures, I was constantly trying to keep my camera properly focused on the action. At times, I was focused on the wrong players and my pictures were worthless. Once, during Tommie Frazier's quarterback sneak for a touchdown, I ran out of film. Yet another time, I shot a picture of Lawrence Phillips flipping into the end zone for a touchdown—but I cut off his legs in the picture. Occasionally, I would take a picture that was sharp and properly focused on the action. What is true of my experience taking photographs is true of sports and life: The "focus" determines the outcome. And Tom Osborne is a good example of someone who kept both sports and life in perspective during the 1995 championship season.

A shoe company has used the slogan "Life is short. Play hard." to sell its sneakers. That's not a bad perspective for athletes. But an even better slogan for the Christian athlete would be "Life is short. Pray hard." Using this slogan, let's think about what we can learn from God's Word and Coach Osborne's season.

LIFE IS SHORT. Psalm 90 compares life to grass that sprouts and withers (v. 5-6) and is soon gone (v. 10). Later in the Bible, James says, "What is your life? You are a mist that appears for a little while and then vanishes" (James 4:14). Since life is so brief, how should we view the present? During the press conference with Tom Osborne following the championship game, he went on to say, "I learned a lot this year. I take my spiritual life very seriously, and there were some times when I ran on empty and relied on my spiritual life."

We can waste our time and energy on what's wrong in

life, or we can focus on the redeeming factors in life. "Consider it pure joy, my brothers, whenever you face trials of many kinds because you know that the testing of your faith develops perseverance" (James 1:2, 3). The Bible is clear—life is too short to waste time reflecting on our negative circumstances.

PRAY HARD. One lesson I learned at the Fiesta Bowl about taking pictures was that the right lens makes the photographer. Without the proper capacity to zoom in on a play or receive the proper amount of light, you can forget taking good pictures. If you want to scope in on the big picture in life, then you'll need a lens that includes prayer and the Bible. Prior to the national championship game, Coach Tom Osborne quoted 2 Timothy 1:7 to his team: "For God did not give us a spirit of timidity," the apostle Paul wrote to Timothy, "but a spirit of power, of love and of self-discipline." While many coaches might be leading their team in a rah-rah victory speech, Coach Osborne was quietly letting his team know where he was coming from. And where he was coming from is a life spent in devotion to God. Life is short. Pray hard!

Coach Dwells in God's Peace

He was without a job, yet he dwelled in God's peace. The 1972 season had come to a close as George Darlington and the entire San Jose football coaching staff had just been fired.

"I had three children and no job," Darlington reflected. "We got one month's salary. That was a time when it should have been extremely stressful. But my wife and I both had tremendous peace concerning God's leading. And one of the verses, which to me is extremely meaningful, is Romans 8:28. 'All things work together for good for those who love God, who are called according to His purpose.'

"It wasn't just words. It really had tremendous meaning because God's promises are true."

Coach Darlington had momentarily lost his ability to provide for his family, yet the Lord sustained him amidst that stressful period with peace, hope, and provision for his needs. Before long, Darlington's coaching career found promise when he was hired onto rookie head coach Tom Osborne's crew in Lincoln as a full-time assistant in 1973.

"There was no way, humanly speaking, that I should have even come to Nebraska. Because Nebraska had come off of such great seasons, they literally could have hired anybody that they had wanted, within reason, to be an assistant coach. And coaches out of work are not exactly hot commodities to go hire. So, the fact that I am here is certainly due to the fact that it was God's desire or will for my life and my wife's life."

George Darlington found tremendous peace from God in spite of his outward circumstances. It was a period when he could have allowed his fears and frustrations to rule over him. In athletics, an unhealthy fear can be perhaps the greatest barrier to achieving success. What effect do our fears have on us? First, fear limits our success and keeps us from reaching our potential. Fear often creates what it fears. The Bible says, "Above all else, guard your heart, for it is the wellspring of life" (Proverbs 4:23). In this passage, Solomon is warning us to be careful about what we think because our lives are shaped by our thoughts. If we focus on what we fear, then it's more likely that what we fear will happen in our lives.

Second, fear destroys our relationships. If we always fear rejection, then it's likely that we'll never develop the type of relationships that God wants for us. Whether it's the relationships within our family or a small group of men or women who support and hold us accountable, the relationships will not grow deep when fear is present.

So what's the answer to conquering our fears? The Bible teaches that we should turn our fears into prayers. "I sought the Lord, and He answered me; He delivered me from all my fears" (Psalm 34:4). David described, in Psalm 27, a time when he was cornered by his enemies. He had every reason to believe that because others had rejected him, he had failed and should quit. But God hadn't rejected David, and he knew that if his confidence was in the Lord, he could overcome his fears. "The Lord is my light and my salvation . . . The Lord is the stronghold of my life . . . Though an army besiege me, my heart will not fear; though war break out against me, even then I will be confident" (Psalm 27:1, 3). God's Word is clear—

freedom from fear begins with a relationship with Him. "So do not fear, for I am with you; do not be dismayed, for I am your God. I will strengthen you and help you; I will uphold you with my righteous right hand" (Isaiah 41:10).

The Apostle Paul offers the same advice: "Do not be anxious about anything, but in everything, by prayer and petition, with thanksgiving, present your requests to God. And the peace of God, which transcends all understanding, will guard your hearts and your minds in Christ Jesus" (Philippians 4:6, 7). A popular sportswear company features the slogan "No Fear" on its apparel. But God's spiritual calm doesn't come from positive thinking, absence of conflict, or in feeling good about ourselves. It comes from knowing God and believing He is in control of our lives, in spite of our circumstances. He is always there. Don't fear. Trust Him.

LESSON TWENTY-SEVEN

Osborne Disciplines His Speech

Thoughtfully chewing his gum, the cool-headed, lanky Tom Osborne would stand along his team's sideline and discuss strategy with his assistant coaches over his headset. The momentum of a game could turn in an instant, and Nebraska's head football coach would regularly have to make split-second decisions amidst the pressure-packed atmosphere. But the independent-spirited man of faith consistently kept his tongue from uttering profanity.

"I tried to eliminate that from my repertoire, so to speak, when I was in high school and junior high school," said Osborne. "I think it's a matter of habit and discipline. And I felt it certainly wasn't going to convey to the young people I was coaching the right message. And then also [during a game on the sideline] I was always focused on what I was going to do next, so ranting and raving and swearing wasn't going to help much. So it became a non-issue after a while. But it's a matter of training and disciplining yourself. I don't think you'd ever find a player who ever heard me use profanity, at least I hope not."

Though he felt many pressures around him, Tom Osborne did not allow them to corrupt his speech. He focused on dealing constructively with problems and avoiding profanity when he was angry. But, sadly, obscenity is incredibly prevalent and accepted in society. And while its use has been common in many locker rooms over the years, its recent overuse in public has dampened its shock value. Like many other offensive behaviors in society, obscenity is normally associated with humor, so we gradually become more tolerant of it. Former Education Secretary William Bennett, crusading to clean up daytime TV, watched two NFL games with his sons. He said the games showed that swearing is "in the mainstream. Now it's over the doggone airwaves." It's not "the end of the world, that three jocks use dirty language," he said. "It's one more notch. . . . Civilizations don't collapse all at once, they do it one degree at a time."

Christians are not always exempt from the problem of profanity or misuse of the tongue—far too often they contribute to it. Here are some warnings from the Bible about the tongue:

"Out of the same mouth come praise and cursing. My brothers, this should not be" (James 3:10).

"The tongue that brings healing is a tree of life, but a deceitful tongue crushes the spirit" (Proverbs 15:4).

"Those whose teeth are swords and whose jaws are set with knives to devour the poor from the earth, the needy from among mankind" (Proverbs 30:14).

Keep in mind that it's not really the tongue that is the message's source. No, the source of the profanity is the heart. "The mouth speaks out of that which fills the heart" (Matthew 12:34). Since the heart is the problem, here are some suggestions for muzzling the tongue:

1. Think before you speak. It's a common saying: "God gave you two ears and one mouth, so listen twice as much as you speak." Emotion is no excuse for letting a few choice four-letter words fly. Athletes need to apply the same self-control used during the game to their postgame interviews. James put it this way: "My dear brothers, take note of this: Everyone should be quick to listen, slow to speak and slow to become angry" (James 1:19). David prayed, "Set a guard over my mouth, O Lord; keep watch over the door of my lips" (Psalm 141:3).

2. Self-control begins with memorizing God's Word. David's strategy for controlling the tongue will work for us today. "I have hidden your word in my heart that I might not sin against you" (Psalm 119:11). James called the tongue a deadly poison and an untamed beast. Want to keep from being flagged for obscenities? Memorize and apply God's Word to your situation. Like pick-and-roll in basketball, it's a simple strategy, but difficult to apply. However, as my basketball coach used to say, "Perfect practice, makes perfect."

LESSON TWENTY-EIGHT

'Unfinished Business'

Following Nebraska's heartbreaking 18-16 loss to Florida State in the 1994 National Championship Orange Bowl, the squad adopted the slogan "Unfinished Business" in their quest to return and win the big game. During the 1994 sultry August two-a-day practices, Nebraska's Memorial Stadium scoreboard flashed "1:16" as a reminder of the game time remaining when the Huskers last held the lead against the Seminoles. That mental image spurred players to excel in the weight room, throughout practices, and during each game.

Thus, on January 1, 1995, undefeated and No. 1 Nebraska faced No. 3 Miami in the National Championship Orange Bowl. The incentive paid off as the Huskers defeated the Hurricanes for the title.

Nebraska players never forgot how close they came to winning it all the previous winter, but they did not let that shortcoming get them down. Rather than live in the heartbreak of that narrow loss to Florida State, players disciplined themselves to get better. And as a result, the team not only returned to the title game, they performed at a superior level in the fourth quarter due to better stamina from conditioning. The game's final score was Nebraska 24, Miami 17.

The memories of that 18-16 loss to Florida State motivated those players, but what drives athletes in general? There are at least three basic philosophies for motivation that apply to any athlete. Let's examine each:

1. Recognition (psychological). The desire for power and prestige motivates many athletes to excel. There is often a sense of power or status from athletic achievement. Some athletes have a strong desire for personal awards or achievement, while still others may be motivated toward team goals. While recognition is a strong motivational force, it depends on circumstances. It's often difficult to control the factors that lead to power or status. Someone who plays on a team that lacks talent has little hope for winning the championship or gaining much attention. And this motivation doesn't always explain why athletes act the way they do. If recognition works all the time, then why do so many powerful achievers still feel unsatisfied?

2. Physical pain and pleasure (physical). Many coaches believe that nothing would get done without their athletes either seeking pleasure or avoiding pain. Examples of this type of motivation are anger, fear, or financial reward. It might be a threat of running sprints or doing pushups, but in each case the athlete responds to the pressure to seek pleasure or avoid pain. Many athletes will do almost anything to avoid a scolding from a coach, but this type of motivational force doesn't explain all behaviors. And it's not always clear which athletes will respond to a particular reward or punishment.

3. Service to God (spiritual). Athletes have a psychological dimension, physical dimension, and spiritual dimension. Each of these dimensions can motivate us to excel. But both the psychological and physical factors often depend on circumstances. You may not always play on the team with the best talent, or possibly you don't respond to intimidation tactics. Nevertheless, here is God's principle for motivation: devotion to God out of love for the development and exercise of Christian character. It's the only acceptable motive for actions that are pleasing to God. "Love the Lord your God with all your heart . . . Love your neighbor as you love yourself" (Matthew 22:37, 39).

Many other factors that motivate us are self-centered, such as money or fame. Our devotion to God should be motivated by our love for Him. The Apostle Paul taught us to express our love for God through our physical abilities, which includes our athletic performance. He wrote, "Therefore, I urge you, brothers, in view of God's mercy, to offer your bodies as living sacrifices, holy and pleasing to God—this is your spiritual act of worship" (Romans 12:1). Because God loves us and because He gave His Son to make our new lives possible, we should joyfully give ourselves as living sacrifices for His service.

LESSON TWENTY-NINE

Preparing For a National Championship

It was the Orange Bowl, but it wasn't the national championship game. It was a quality win over a respected opponent. Nevertheless, it felt like a non-game as the Huskers had spent their last three bowl trips playing for the title. Even the attendance on that final night of 1996 was at least 20,000 shy of being a sellout. Former Nebraska football coach Tom Osborne recounted the perspective his sixth-ranked team faced following a 41-21 victory over No. 10 Virginia Tech in the Orange Bowl. Next year things would be much different. Nebraska would be a contender for the 1997 national title.

"There was a resolve that on January 2, 1998, we were going to be in the big game," Osborne said.

Players demonstrated that fierce commitment, not only on the playing field, but during the off-season as well.

"One time that summer, I happened to be walking by the [practice] field," recalled Osborne, "and one of our senior players sees a guy in a drill 20 yards away who wasn't working very hard. This guy runs 20 yards and tackles the guy in sweat clothes in July. I called him over, and I said, 'We don't do those kinds of things.' But that was an example of the commitment that was there."

Thus, his team returned to form. Tom Osborne went on to close out his 25-year head coaching career as his team posted a 42-17 thumping over No. 3 Tennessee in the national championship game.

"And so it wasn't by accident that we ended up where we were on January 2, 1998."

As training in athletics is crucial for success, how much more critical is spiritual training for life. God commands us to be constantly training ourselves toward godliness. But spiritual growth isn't hereditary. It takes commitment. Perhaps you were raised by godly parents. Their influence through training you to be godly had much more to do with your character development than your bloodline.

The Apostle Paul didn't take his spiritual son Timothy's godliness for granted. Although Timothy was his teammate for many years, Paul thought it was necessary to encourage him to train himself to be godly. "Have nothing to do with godless myths and old wives' tales; rather, train yourself to be godly" (1 Timothy 4:7).

When Paul instructed Timothy to train himself in godliness, he used a term familiar to athletes and coaches. The verb that some versions of the Bible translate as "exercise," "train," or "discipline," originally referred to athletes who competed in the sports of their day. Later, the word "train" meant the training or disciplining of either the body or the mind in a skill. For us to understand how to train ourselves to be godly, we need to understand three basic questions:

1. Who is responsible for my training? (Train yourself.) Paul said, "Train yourself." Of course, none of us can grow spiritually without God's help, but Paul's point was that Timothy must work at pursuing his training. God was certainly at work in his life, but we can't be lazy in our approach to spiritual growth. No Olympic athlete can afford to simply relax his/her training schedule a few weeks before his/her event.

Neither can we pray, "Lord, make me godly," and expect God to instantly turn us into some spiritual giant.

2. What is the goal of my training? (Devotion to God.) Paul also reminds Timothy that the goal of training himself for godliness was growth in his personal life, not his ministry. Paul had instructed Timothy earlier to be concerned with the growth of his ministry, but here Paul wants Timothy to be concerned with his own devotion to God. Paul's instruction to Timothy is a good reminder for us. We should be more concerned with personal devotion to God, rather than our amount of Christian activity.

3. What do we need to train properly?

- Use the right equipment (Bible).
- Practice godliness (no short cuts).
- Learn from a personal trainer (be trained by godly men and women).

LESSON THIRTY

Former Husker Confronts Addiction

Nearly 20 years of addiction to drugs and alcohol came to a halt when pro football veteran Bob Newton heeded a coach's advice to receive treatment in a 12-step program. The former Husker All-American offensive lineman and member of the 1970 Nebraska national championship team recalled the admonition of the former Boston Breakers' head coach.

"My coach, Dick Coury, said, and I'll never forget it, 'Unless you get some help for your drinking problem, you're going to end up on skid row.' "

And with a repentant heart and resolve before God, Newton confronted the sinful habits of his life and made necessary lifestyle changes.

Prior to admitting his chemical dependency, Newton made excuses for his behavior.

"During [my last] training camp, my intoxication caused me to miss practice. I told them I would quit drinking on my own, which was always the great alibi."

And with that, the offensive lineman was cut from the team shortly thereafter. Dick Coury's warning that he would end up on skid row helped wake Newton to his senses. But Newton could not change or get help until he admitted he had a problem. Bob Newton not only had a drinking problem, he had a sin problem. And likewise, we cannot come before a Holy God without admitting our sin and accepting His forgiveness through Christ.

First, let's define sin. It's not a word that we use every day, although we see it in our lives and in the lives of those around us. The word "sin" is an archery term. It means, "missing the mark." The "sin-mark" is the distance between the bulls-eye on a target and the place the arrow hits. When the Bible says we have sinned, it's describing our missing the mark of God's perfection. It's falling short of His glory. Sin offends our holy God and separates us from Him. Just as oil cannot mix with water, sin cannot mix with God.

Now that we have defined "sin," let's think about the message God sent about the consequences of sin through His messenger Isaiah. "But your iniquities have separated you from your God; your sins have hidden His face from you, so that He will not hear" (Isaiah 59:2). Now let's examine God's view of sin:

1. Sin cannot be ignored. Many in our society turn their backs on sin, hoping not to notice the damage it does or the offense it is to a holy God. Experts often argue about kids being desensitized to violence by watching too much television. Is it possible that Christians have become desensitized toward sin? Because we watch it on TV, see it at the movies, or hear about it in the locker room, have we gotten to the point of turning our backs on sin? Jesus didn't ignore sin. In fact, as the Pharisees discovered, Jesus confronted their pride and selfish ambition. "Woe to you, teachers of the law and Pharisees, you hypocrites! You clean the outside of the cup and dish, but inside they are full of greed and self-indulgence" (Matthew 23:25).

2. Sin cannot be excused. We live in a society that views nearly everyone as a victim. It's no longer just the person who was violated by the crime, but now it's also the violator who has become the victim.

Jesus didn't excuse the righteous when they neglected to help the poor. "They also will answer, 'Lord, when did we see you hungry or thirsty or a stranger or needing clothes or sick or in prison, and did not help you?' He will reply, 'I tell you the truth, whatever you did not do for one of the least of these, you did not do for me.' Then they will go away to eternal punishment, but the righteous to eternal life" (Matthew 25:44-46).

3. Sin cannot be tolerated. Perhaps the only view in our society that is not tolerated is no-tolerance. The only person not tolerated is often the person who believes in moral absolutes. When the money changers in the temple interfered with worshiping God, Jesus would not tolerate their sin, so He went on the offensive by clearing the temple of their presence.

Drug and alcohol abuse took their toll on Bob Newton's life. Yet, Bob, who now works full-time helping others overcome similar addictions, was not beyond God's saving grace. Bob Newton chose to confront the sin in his life and accept the Lord's forgiveness through Christ's death on the cross and resurrection from the grave. Whether or not you have ever given in to the false allure of drugs or alcohol, everyone battles temptation in some form. If you are struggling with the temptation to take drugs or alcohol, find someone you can talk to who can help you overcome it. Don't face that battle alone. Though being tempted is not a sin, giving in to it is. Do you consistently allow the Lord to deal with you in the sinful areas in your life so that you can live the Christian life more abundantly?

LESSON THIRTY-ONE

Newton's Road to Recovery

For former Husker All-American and pro football veteran Bob Newton, the road to recovery from chemical dependency was a narrow one. It meant a strict commitment to abstinence and a dependence upon God's grace and strength. As he went through a 12-step program, Newton recommitted his life to the Lord.

"One of the steps of the 12-step program to help you recover from alcoholism is that you have to turn your life and your will over to the care of God. That is what started my path back to the Lord, getting the alcohol and the other drugs out of me and getting my head cleared up. I saw that I had to replace this lifestyle with the Lord. There was a void I had tried to fill up with booze, drugs, and football. I had to fill that up with my relationship with the Lord."

Newton did recover. And since the mid-1980s, he has served full-time to help others find victory over substance abuse as well.

Bob Newton's choice to stay sober has meant taking life one day at a time. But you don't have to be addicted to drugs to face difficult choices in life. Like Bob, many Christians must choose which road they will follow.

One day as I watched CBS's coverage of the NCAA men's basketball tournament, I thought about the theme used to open each show, "The Road to the Final Four." For Bob Newton or any of us, the theme could be "The Road to Eternal Life." You see, each of us, too, will choose daily which road to travel. Which road will you choose? The Fellowship of Christian Athletes has developed a model for challenging athletes to take the high road. Their "One Way 2 Play—Drug Free!" program encourages athletes to daily choose the high road.

Faith in Jesus Christ (High Road versus Low Road). First, let's define the high road. For the Christian, the high road involves faithfully choosing God's way instead of man's way. Faith doesn't mean we disconnect our brains and ignore our responsibility to think. Instead, it's the idea of recognizing that each of us has a limited ability to think and reason. The Bible puts it this way: "As the heavens are higher than the earth, so are my ways higher than your ways and my thoughts than your thoughts" (Isaiah 55:9). That's why we need to study God's playbook, the Bible. Without God's direction, each of us is limited to our own understanding. This was Solomon's point when he wrote, "Trust in the Lord with all your heart and lean not on your own understanding; in all your ways acknowledge Him, and He will make your paths straight" (Proverbs 3:5, 6). Of course, none of us can lean on God's wisdom without first trusting in Jesus Christ for our salvation. It's only through a relationship with the living God that we can choose the high road.

Commitment to say "no" to alcohol and other drugs (Take the high road). There's no way to stick with a commitment or steer clear of problem areas without God's power. Recognize that you can't do it on your own. Only God can provide the power! "But you will receive power when the Holy Spirit comes on you; and you will be my witnesses in Jerusalem, and in all Judea and

Samaria, and to the ends of the earth" (Acts 1:8). The person who flip-flops between God's way and his/her own wisdom is called double-minded in James 1:8.

Accountability to one another (Help to stay on the high road). Once you're part of God's team, then you need to be accountable to your teammates. No quarterback can run the option without the cooperation of his line. "Two are better than one, because they have a good return for their work: If one falls down, his friend can help him up. But pity the man who falls and has no one to help him up!" (Ecclesiastes 4:9-10).

LESSON THIRTY-TWO

State Stunned by Death

"If you had somebody you wanted your son to be like, Brook would be a good place to start," Nebraska coach Tom Osborne stated only short hours following quarterback Brook Berringer's tragic death in a plane crash. "He was one of those guys who stood for all the right things. Brook was a great guy. He deserves to be remembered."

As a Husker, Berringer played a key role in directing Nebraska to the 1994 national title. During that year, the Goodland, Kan., native bravely faced the adversity of playing during three games with a partially collapsed lung as he went on to march the team through an undefeated season. In 1995 he played sparingly behind starter Tommie Frazier. Berringer was a young man with great character and ability who had everything to live for. But on Thursday, April 18, 1996, 22-year-old Berringer and his passenger, Tobey Lake, brother of Brook's girlfriend, took off in a 1946 Piper Cub from a private rural airstrip in Raymond, Neb. They left at approximately 2:30 p.m. for what was to have been a brief ride. The plane reportedly ascended to approximately 250 feet, stalled, fell into a nose-dive and crashed in a field.

Brook's death happened the same day he was to join a handful of teammates and coaches in speaking at the state Fellowship of Christian Athletes banquet in Lincoln. Fans and players at the dinner, mourning his tragic passing, hugged one another. Brook's passing also preceded the National Football League draft by two days. But amidst that tragedy, many have come to a saving faith in Jesus Christ as a result of Brook's powerful Christian testimony.

I was shocked. Only a few hours had passed since Brook's plane crashed when I heard about his death at that April 1996 FCA banquet. I was so surprised I don't even remember who told me the news. Any death is tragic, yet whenever a young person suddenly dies, it's hard to accept.

Most Nebraska football fans were very familiar with Brook. However, only a few people outside the state knew much about Brook besides what they saw on the football field. I think it's important for me to reflect on what we should all know about Brook Berringer.

At the FCA banquet, Coach Osborne said, "If you had somebody that you wanted your son to be like, it would be Brook. He was just a good guy. He was one of those people who stood for all the right things."

Two of Brook's former teammates who spoke at the FCA banquet talked about Brook. Aaron Graham, a team co-captain at center, said, "We lost a great person who was a great friend." Tony Veland, a senior safety, said, "Brook was a great teammate, a great friend, and a great person. All his teammates are hurting."

Brook was obviously a great player and person. But, most important of all, he was a Christian. Just a few short months prior to that plane crash he made a decision that changed not only his life, but also his destiny. Art Lindsay, who spoke for Brook at the banquet, shared how Brook committed his life to Christ.

"I met Brook several years ago when I heard his name mentioned at the football stadium. I had never heard of him before, but for some reason the Lord placed it on my heart to pray for him. During the next several years, we became good friends. This past August, I asked him if he had ever put his faith in Jesus Christ. When he asked me what that meant, I told him. I shared that God's Son Jesus came to earth and died for each of us so we might have eternal life. I asked him if he wanted to take that step of faith by placing his trust in Jesus Christ. He explained that he had never understood what people meant by a relationship with Christ. But now that he understood it, he wanted this relationship for himself. We prayed together, and Brook joined God's team. During the past few months, we spent much time together praying and studying the Bible. When I asked him where he wanted to be in five years, he responded by telling me that he only cared about growing closer to Jesus Christ in this newly found spiritual relationship. There was no mention of the upcoming NFL draft or which team he might like to play on. Clearly, Brook had become a child of God."

Brook's untimely death has been a wake-up call for many. Salvation is the single most important decision in life. Yet, if we are not careful, we'll put it off. Fortunately, Brook didn't delay his decision to accept Jesus Christ as Lord and Savior of his life. Take a moment to read the following Scriptures. Don't postpone making the same decision.

1. We are lost (Romans 3:10-18).
2. We are sinful (Romans 3:23).
3. We need God's help (Romans 6:23).
4. God will forgive our sins if we repent (1 John 1:9).
5. Christ died for us (John 3:16).
6. Heaven is available (John 14:1-3).
7. We must believe (John 11:25-26).

8. Salvation is a gift that we can't earn (Ephesians 2:8-9).

When Brook Berringer joined the Nebraska football team, he became a hero for thousands of fans. And while most fans will remember him as a part of the back-to-back national championship teams, I'll remember him as my teammate in Christ. "Therefore, if anyone is in Christ, he is a new creation; the old has gone, the new has come!" (2 Corinthians 5:17).

Freshman Quarterback Controls Anger

It had been an uphill battle on the undefeated, No. 1-ranked Kansas State's home field, but the eleventh-ranked Huskers clung to hope during a Nov. 14, 1998, matchup. Trailing 34-30 with 2:40 left in the game, it was fourth and eight. Freshman quarterback Eric Crouch dropped back, looking for a receiver. But defender Travis Ochs penetrated the line and grabbed Crouch's face mask, pulling him backwards to the turf. Officials missed the call, which would have resulted in a 15-yard penalty and automatic first down near mid-field.

The no-call face mask was a critical moment in deciding the game's outcome; nevertheless, Crouch did not unleash his anger upon the referee. The freshman demonstrated the maturity of a senior by controlling his temper.

"Whenever you think of a player in college athletics or wherever, the first thing that comes to mind is what their character is like," Crouch said later in response to the official's no-call. "When that face-mask happened at Kansas State, it was pretty blatant. And I thought that it should've been called a penalty. When it didn't get called, I wasn't upset because of the game, but there's the injury factor in that. If they don't make that call and I get seriously injured, then the referees are dealing with some pretty serious stuff right there. When that play happened, I also thought about, 'What's going to be the best thing for me to do? Am I going to get up in the ref's face?' I didn't think that would be the best thing to do.

"I think the best way to handle any situation, for that matter, is to try to be as calm as you can. Sometimes that's hard to do, especially in a situation like that at Kansas State where I almost broke my neck. But you have to deal with things like that."

The manner in which Eric Crouch handled his anger is exemplary. How can we overcome anger? Whenever our anger is based on selfishness or wrong motives, it becomes sin. Here are several practical ways to deal with your anger:

1. **Understand why you get angry.** Most of the time, anger is based on selfishness. Think about it. Why does a baseball player throw his bat in disgust after he strikes out? What ticks off a basketball player when an official's call goes against him? How about a football player who's benched for making a mistake during the game? Usually, anger is motivated by frustration, insecurity, and personal injury. Recognize the source of your anger and realize that it's wrong. "A man's wisdom gives him patience" (Proverbs 19:11).

2. **Stop and think before reacting.** Most athletes would guess that the leg muscle is their most powerful muscle. However, it's the muscle in their mouth that can do the most damage and is the most difficult to control. Learning to keep the tongue in check will literally turn away wrath. "A gentle answer turns away wrath, but a harsh word stirs up anger" (Proverbs 15:1). And on the flip side, a lack of self-control can be trouble. "He who guards his mouth and his tongue, guards his soul from troubles" (Proverbs 21:23).

3. **Overlook petty disagreements.** Pro sports, particularly the National Basketball Association, have problems with players disrespecting the officials. No doubt referees in the NBA may need to do a better job of dealing with players' tantrums, but most of the blame falls on the

players. "The beginning of strife is like letting out water, so abandon the quarrel before it breaks out" (Proverbs 17:14).

4. Don't hang out with angry people. While it's not necessarily practical to avoid contact with a teammate who is prone to temper tantrums, it is possible to limit your time around those with this problem. If you hang around people who are angry, you know what happens. You become angry and negative. "Do not associate with a man given to anger or go with a hot-tempered man, lest you learn his ways and find a snare for yourself" (Proverbs 22:24, 25).

LESSON THIRTY-FOUR

Osborne Inducted Into Hall of Fame

Following 25 years of unparalleled success as Nebraska's legendary head coach, Tom Osborne was inducted into the College Football Hall of Fame December 9, 1998. The 62-year-old Hastings, Neb., native recorded a career record of 255-49-3 with 25-straight bowl appearances and a 60-3 record during his final five years that included three national titles. The Hall of Fame even waived a three-year waiting period to admit Osborne following his retirement.

Barry Switzer, a former rival skipper at the University of Oklahoma, ranked Osborne among the greatest coaches of all time.

"Tom's in there with [Frank] Leahy, [Knute] Rockne, all those guys. He's all about college football. Tom casts his shadow as far as those guys and not because he was taller than them. He was just huge."

What an honor for Tom Osborne! Not only to be inducted into the Hall of Fame, but to be named less than a year following his retirement. Can you imagine joining the likes of Knute Rockne, Bud Wilkinson, or Bear Bryant?

Getting into the College Football Hall of Fame takes a certain level of achievement by a coach or athlete. For example, it may be somebody with a great winning record or someone who rushed for so many yards or recorded so many tackles. Induction demands an incredibly high level of excellence and perfection.

But what about God's Hall of Faith? Are the entry

requirements different? Do we have to be perfect to get into it? God's Hall of Faith doesn't require a certain "type" of person. Any type will work. God didn't limit the exercise of faith to only ministers. Check out a list of different "types" in Hebrews chapter 11. It lists a farmer, businessman, homemaker, shepherd, king, songwriter, judge, and politician. Even Rahab, a former prostitute, made the list.

Most Hall of Fame candidates have great records. Tom Osborne averaged more than ten wins a season and won three national championships. The legendary Knute Rockne of Notre Dame boasted the highest winning percentage of all time. The former skipper of the Alabama Crimson Tide, Paul "Bear" Bryant, won 323 games during his 38-year head coaching career.

Again, God's Hall of Faith is different. The inductees don't necessarily have a special record. And they're far from perfect. In fact, most of them had a weakness that God dealt with. For example: Moses murdered a man; Rahab was a prostitute; and Noah got drunk after the flood.

Aren't you glad that God's Hall of Faith isn't limited to a few spiritual giants? The people in Hebrews were like you and me. They believed God existed and trusted Him when faced with the tough circumstances. The writer of Hebrews was trying to convey this point: Faith is possible in anyone's life. You have the potential to one day storm into the Hall of Faith.

LESSON THIRTY-FIVE

Frazier Won't Go Down

At its annual ESPY sports award celebration, ESPN cable sports network named it the 1995 College Football Play of the Year. To Husker fans, it is simply referred to as "The Run."

Leading No. 2 Florida 42-18 late in the third quarter of the Jan. 2, 1996, Fiesta Bowl national championship game, Nebraska's offense lined up over the ball at the 25-yard line. Husker quarterback Tommie Frazier took the snap and darted right behind his offensive line. Frazier faked to trailing back Clinton Childs and charged upfield, only to be met by several would-be tacklers. But Frazier tucked the ball inside and kept moving forward. Four Gator defenders clung to him together inside the Husker 40, but the runner-up for the 1995 Heisman Trophy kept pressing ahead. Frazier broke through as Florida players fell away. A lone Floridian cornerback, Fred Weary, lunged for him but clung momentarily in vain as Frazier sprinted free en route to a 75-yard touchdown run. Frazier looked over his shoulder in laughing disbelief as he crossed the end zone. Perhaps Weary's last name was symbolic of how the Gator defense felt as they watched red jersey No. 15 break through eight would-be tacklers.

Perseverance and determination sum up Frazier's tough 75-yard touchdown run. In the Christian life, believers face adversity and things that could pull them down. But as Frazier clung to the ball and kept his legs going forward, we must cling to our faith and press on.

Perseverance and determination are two important character qualities needed by every Christian. The spiritual life of a Christian is much more like a cross-country run than a sprint. I don't know how many times I've seen a young believer in Christ start fast and fizzle out before getting anywhere near the finish line. A marathon runner needs to develop the second wind to make it over the long haul. He needs to develop the staying power to hang tough.

As a Christian, you don't need to gut it out on your own. Faith is a matter of relying on God for your strength. God can do amazing things through us, by His power. Jesus said, ". . . apart from me you can do nothing" (John 15:5b). The Apostle Paul said, "Now to Him who is able to do immeasurably more than all we ask or imagine, according to His power that is at work within us" (Ephesians 3:20).

You have a choice. You can choose to gut out the spiritual race on your own and burn out. Or you can choose to depend on His power and finish the race with a kick. Remember, when you are faced with an impossible situation, stretch out your courage, hang tough, and depend on Him.

LESSON THIRTY-SIX

Faithful Football Fans

Fans of the Big Red can be found nationwide. The number of Husker faithful likely rivals all programs across the country, including Notre Dame. With legendary coaches such as the late Bob Devaney and Tom Osborne, the football program has recorded long-term consistency over the decades. Trademarks of the Husker tradition include annual winning seasons since 1962, consecutive nine-plus win seasons dating back to 1969, consecutive bowl trips since '69, over 200-straight sellout home games, five national championships, over 80 players who have earned first-team All-American status, and over 40 players named Academic All-American.

Though it can be fun to cheer for a consistent winner, athletes, coaches, and teams can sadly become idols for many fans. In the Bible, John warns us about idols: "Dear children, keep yourselves from idols" (1 John 5:21). Almost anything can qualify as an idol. You can make an idol out of anything or anyone. It might be your sport, a car, an award, a job, or even Nebraska football.

Now, before you tear down your Big Red poster, realize that there is nothing necessarily wrong with college football in and of itself. To possess sports posters and other memorabilia is not wrong, but to let them possess us is wrong. It would be nice and neat if there was a list of things not to buy. It doesn't work that way. In fact, it's the good things I have the most trouble keeping in perspective.

I've never really had to struggle with worshiping evil people or things. It's the good role models or things in life that more easily take the spotlight off God.

Jesus Christ needs to be the center of your life. It's easy to allow other things to take His place, but He wants to be first! The Bible says, "And He is the head of the body, the church; He is the beginning and the firstborn from among the dead, so that in everything He might have the supremacy" (Colossians 1:18). So what takes first place in your life? Is it your new car? How about your body? Anything, I repeat, *anything* that replaces God at the center of your life is wrong!

Is God opposed to idols? Yes! Does God care about being first in your life? You bet. C'mon, Christian, let's get our priorities straight. If there's one thing God will not tolerate, it's not being at the top of the list.

Huskers Demonstrate Maturity

Following a narrow 18-16 loss to Florida State in the Jan. 1, 1994, Orange Bowl national championship, players resolved that the title would not slip from their grasp the following season. And the most notable difference between the 1993 and '94 Huskers was maturity.

Receivers' coach Ron Brown recalled how many players lost their poise late in that contest with Florida State.

"When our kicker, Byron Bennett, booted the field goal with 1:16 left in the game, putting us ahead 16-15, pure bedlam ripped across our sideline. It appeared to be an uncontrollable situation. Players were running out to the field from our sideline screaming, hugging, and pointing at the Florida State sideline. Being excited is one thing, but losing total control is quite another."

The Seminoles, starting from their own 35-yard line, marched downfield behind Heisman Trophy-winning quarterback Charlie Ward. The drive culminated in a game-winning Scott Bentley 22-yard field goal with 21 seconds left.

A year later, things were different. The 1994 Huskers were better conditioned and a bit wiser. With 2:46 remaining, NU fullback Cory Schlesinger exploded for a 14-yard touchdown. The score put Nebraska in front 24-17. "Our sideline was much different than a year ago," said Brown. "This sideline was calm and confident. I looked up at [junior wingback] Clester [Johnson] as he kept shaking his head saying, 'It's not over.' This certainly was championship maturity."

Nothing slows down a team like a lack of consistency. The 1994 Nebraska national championship team consistently kept its poise throughout the season and bowl game. Every coach looks for mature consistency. If a team doesn't have it, they struggle. It's the glue that holds a team together over the long haul. Any team can put together a streak. Even the weakest of teams can win several games in a row. It's the great teams that practice well and play well consistently. A 60-3 record with three national championships over five years in the 1990s didn't happen to the Cornhuskers by chance. It happened because they consistently strove to be the best in practice and during each game.

God also looks for consistency. It's a mark of maturity. Let's take a quiz. Keep your eyes on your own papers.

1. How often did you say something this week that you shouldn't have?

2. How often did you read your Bible this week?

3. Did you pray each day?

4. Did you show others that you loved and cared about them?

5. Did you hang out anywhere you shouldn't have?

Okay, how did you do? If you're like me, you probably feel at least a little bit guilty. It's not easy to be consistent, is it? How do you become more consistent in your spiritual life? Spend time with God. It's really that simple to concentrate on Him and do what you are capable of doing.

Take time to develop habits that will help you be more consistent in your spiritual walk. It's true: "Sow a thought, reap an act; sow an act, reap a habit; sow a habit, reap a character; sow a character, reap a destiny."

Timothy offers valuable advice on how to become more consistent in your spiritual life: "All Scripture is God-breathed and is useful for teaching, rebuking, correction and training in righteousness, so that the man of God may be thoroughly equipped for every good work" (2 Timothy 3:16, 17).

Don't be a rookie in your spiritual life. Develop a consistent spiritual life by making it a habit to read and apply the Bible. Believe me, it's important to God. You can count on it.

Demanding Fans

Scott Frost bore high expectations from demanding fans before he ever wore Husker red. The quarterback from Wood River, Neb., was touted a prep All-American and top-rate passer. The Nebraska high school all-class state champion shot putter took his strong arm to Stanford as he sought the tutelage of coach Bill Walsh, former mastermind behind three of the San Francisco 49ers' Super Bowl wins. Following his sophomore season, Frost returned to the university of his home state following Walsh's resignation. In 1996, the 6-foot-3 signal caller followed top-notch quarterbacks Tommie Frazier and the late Brook Berringer, who had helped lead NU to consecutive national championships. Many fans, who once felt betrayed that Frost had left his home state for a school on the west coast, now heaped unrealistic expectations upon the new starting quarterback.

For Frost, the 1996 19-0 loss at Arizona State and the boos he received during a 38-24 '97 regular season victory over Central Florida in Lincoln were, perhaps, symbolic of his lowest points.

"That was a very difficult time for me," Frost said of the devastation in Tempe, Ariz. "That was probably the most painful game I had to endure in my career, but it was also one of the most important because it put things in perspective for me."

Thus, on Sept. 29, 1997, when seventh-ranked NU played at then No. 2 Washington, Frost truly felt the pressure to perform. "At that point there was a lot of burden on my shoulders, I felt, because there wasn't really anyone behind me, including a lot of my own fans. It was a time when I could've given up, I could've been down on myself."

But the determined quarterback persevered. Frost finished the game with two rushing touchdowns.

Thus, when No. 2 Nebraska faced third-ranked Tennessee in the Orange Bowl, with the national media projecting virtually no chance of earning a share of the title with No. 1 Michigan, Frost was prepared to handle the pressure. And the Huskers did perform at a high level, pounding the Volunteers 42-17 for first place in the coaches' poll.

"I had already gone through some tough times, and I honestly believe it was to get me ready for things like this. This was another big test and another time when the odds were against us. But after all I had gone through, I think I had developed the strength of character to be able to help lead the team to that win."

There was not much Scott Frost could have done about the fans' expectations during his seasons at Nebraska's helm. The pressure to perform well without failing can be very unhealthy for those who live under someone else's expectations.

At all levels, fans demand high performance. It starts in Little League and never ends. It can consume those who watch and those who play.

Expectations have a way of bringing out the worst in us, rather than the best. It seems to depend on who sets the standard. Are such expectations fair? Unbiased? Realistic? If not, then expectations work against us, rather than for us.

What kind of expectations do you set for yourself? What kind of expectations do you set for others? While you can't do much about what others say and think, you can do something about the way you set expectations for others. Give others a chance to be themselves. Don't try to make them into your own image. There are many personalities. Be thankful that God made you the way you are and the same for your friends.

The Bible says, "Accept one another, then, just as Christ accepted you, in order to bring praise to God" (Romans 15:7).

For Christians, such acceptance can be tough. Most churches are made up of people who only accept others based on what they do or don't do. This list of "do's and don'ts" or expectations is not biblical, but cultural. In other words, expectations might be based on how we dress, speak, or look, rather than how we treat one another.

Let's pray that we can begin to accept others based on who they are in Christ, not on what they can do for us. Nothing is more frustrating than trying to live up to higher expectations than we can handle. Don't boo those who need love and acceptance. We already spend too much time scrutinizing one another and not enough time accepting each other.

The longer I live, the more I'm convinced that unrealistic expectations in the spiritual world lead only to frustration and stress, not to Christian maturity.

LESSON THIRTY-NINE

Huskers Miss Titles

Forty-eight seconds remained in the Jan. 2, 1984, national championship Orange Bowl, and No. 1 Nebraska trailed No. 5 Miami 31-30. The Husker offense had just scored a 24-yard touchdown on fourth down. A successful two-point conversion would cap a perfect season and clinch the national title.

Husker quarterback Turner Gill took the snap. Nebraska All-American wingback Irving Fryar sped out as a decoy receiver. I-back Jeff Smith had a step on defender strong safety Ken Calhoun at the goal line. Gill fired to Smith, but the ball never reached his hands as Calhoun reached and deflected it. Smith strained futilely to grasp the leather ball as it bounced off his chest like a bullet and trailed off into the night sky an incompletion.

A decade later on Jan. 1, 1994, No. 2 Nebraska's offense faced the same Orange Bowl end zone, trailing top-ranked Florida State 18-16 with one second remaining. Husker kicker Byron Bennett lined up for the potential game-winning 45-yard field goal. The placeholder reeled in the center snap and placed it for Bennett. The kick sailed wide left as the previously undefeated Cornhuskers saw another national title slip through their fingers on the same field.

"I laid back, put my hands over my eyes and just started crying," said David Seizys, Nebraska's holder for PATs and field goals. "I knew it [our loss] was for a reason, but it just hurt."

A season of commitment and a lifetime of dreams shattered in an instant. For those two Nebraska teams, the pain of losing a national championship by one imperfect play ran deep. Losses can be emotionally draining and hurtful; nevertheless, it's all in your perspective. Though Cornhusker All-American linebacker Trev Alberts was frustrated by the narrow loss to Florida State, he held his head high.

"I feel like we're champions," he stated following the '94 Orange Bowl. "There's not a frown on my face."

The missed field goal attempt did not shake Coach Tom Osborne's contented demeanor.

"The main thing to me is that we played well enough to win the championship. The ball just didn't happen to go through the uprights. We were at the top level of college football. And there has to be a certain amount of dedication and commitment to excellence to do that. Winning or losing isn't as critical as playing well." Disappointing, yes, but it was also a time when those individuals took pride in a job well done, in spite of the loss.

Can you imagine the disappointment that Olympic athletes feel when they fail? After all, they train for four years for a competition which may last only seconds. Then to lose by a fraction of a second or to win against the world's best must bring to the surface a lot of emotions. It reminds me of the lead into ABC TV's *Wide World of Sports*: "The thrill of victory and the agony of defeat." First, you see several athletes celebrate their victories. Then, you see the poor skier crash and burn. These two video clips sum up the emotions every athlete feels after competition, even if only for a brief moment.

How do you deal with disappointments? As I watched the other athletes compete during the Olympics, I noticed that some got angry, others cried, and a few were emotionless when they lost. Can you lose and not be upset or hopelessly disappointed?

The book of James helps us understand how to respond to disappointment. "Consider it pure joy, my brothers, whenever you face trails of many kinds, because you know that the testing of your faith develops endurance" (James 1:2).

It's important to understand two things about troubles from this verse. First, disappointments are inevitable. It's true in sports, isn't it? You just can't win every time you compete. Second, disappointment has purpose. The testing of our faith produces endurance. So God is teaching us endurance and helping us grow in our faith.

The point is not to pretend to be happy about our disappointments, but to have a positive attitude about them. The Bible teaches that there is a difference between joy and happiness. Happiness is a feeling, but joy is an attitude. You see, happiness depends on circumstances, but joy is always a choice we can make. We can't avoid pain and disappointment, but we can choose joy over misery.

The next time you lose or are disappointed by something, remember, God is helping you grow in your faith and giving you the option to choose joy.

LESSON FORTY

Huskers Win Game of the Century

It was November 25, 1971, the day of what would be the most talked about game in Nebraska football history. The defending national champion Huskers edged No. 2 Oklahoma 35-31 in Norman, Okla. All-American running back Jeff Kinney finished that memorable afternoon with 171 yards rushing and four touchdowns.

"It was nip and tuck all day," recalled Kinney. "We didn't know if we were going to win it or not. It was emotional after we won the game. The excitement was generated by the crowd coming out on the field."

Several thousand screaming fans converged on Lincoln's airport upon the return of their conquering heroes from Oklahoma.

"It was just a neat experience to see the people of Nebraska so excited, so involved in that event. I remember coming back from the Oklahoma game, and 30,000 people came out to the airport. It was just a fun time," said Kinney.

Everyone loves a winner. We love to praise the deeds of athletes, don't we? We praise them for what they have done and what they will do in the future. Bedlam exploded across the Nebraska plains following the Cornhuskers' victory in the Game of the Century.

Praise is a natural ingredient in sports. Fans praised Jeff Kinney for his four touchdowns. People praised 1972

Husker Heisman Trophy-winning wingback Johnny "The Jet" Rodgers for his brilliant athletic ability. But as football fans praise their team for its amazing feats, how much more should Christians praise God for all He has done!

If we can spend the time and energy praising sports teams and heroes, why not praise God? He not only expects it, He demands it. Listen to what one writer in the Bible had to say about praise:

"Let everything that has breath praise the Lord. Praise the Lord" (Psalm 150:6).

What can you praise God for today? After all, if 30,000 Cornhusker fans could jubilantly praise their team, can we do any less for God? And don't stop at praising Him for only the good things. Praise Him during the good and bad times as well—even when we're hurt, depressed, and confused. It is during times like those that we need to praise God more than ever. Praise is both a response to God and also a step toward seeing God make changes in your life. You see, as you praise Him for what He has done and will do in your life, it frees you up to depend on Him. As you depend on Him, you become less dependent on yourself.

Have you praised God today? I hope you will daily look for reasons to praise Him. Because as you praise Him, you'll begin to see just how much He loves and cares for you.

LESSON FORTY-ONE

All-American Shares 'Greatest' Memory

It was November 11, 1978, and fourth-ranked Nebraska had just pulled the unbelievable on its home field with a 17-14 win over No. 1 Oklahoma. The Cornhuskers had not beaten the Sooners since the '71 Game of the Century in Norman. But this team was on a mission and was riding a nine-game winning streak. Husker senior All-American defensive end George Andrews finished the game with seven tackles, including two for 16 yards in losses.

Reporters flanked the team's defensive captain following the upset. One television journalist asked the 6'4", 225-pound defensive lineman what the victory meant to him.

"An announcer asked me after the game, 'Is this the greatest day in your life?'" recalled Andrews. "And I was able to share that it wasn't because it would pass. But I said I had a relationship that would last for eternity. It was a special opportunity to share my faith."

It's not unusual to see an athlete on television thank God for a victory or see players huddled together in prayer following a game. Though that has not always been a common sight, in many sports the Christian faith has become somewhat accepted in the locker room and on the field. Most college football programs have chapel services before their games. More players than ever are involved with Fellowship of Christian Athletes, Pro Athletes Outreach, Athletes in Action, and other sports-related ministries.

The national media and American Civil Liberties Union, among others, have questioned the appropriateness of prayer in the locker room or on the field. Some think Christians have gone too far. While believers see opportunity, non-believers see red, or in some cases, Bible verses written on huge banners draped over stadium stands.

But what's the real issue? For Christians, it seems to be obedience. After all, God has told us to reach the world with the gospel (which includes sports fans).

Jesus said, "Go therefore and make disciples of all nations . . ." (Matthew 28:18).

Jesus wasn't giving us an option but a command to share our faith with others. Maybe you're uncomfortable with sharing your faith with others. Maybe when you think of witnessing, you think of an evangelist, and you know you're anything but an evangelist. God gives each of us different gifts, but with the same responsibility. You may not be as outspoken or bold about your faith as some who receive great media attention. And yet, God will give you opportunities to share, if you're faithful.

God doesn't necessarily ask you to lead thousands to Christ, though He might. He does command you to sincerely share what He has done in your life. You know something? God may ask you to pray on a sideline, hang a sign at a game, or pray in the end zone. But don't count on it. More often than not, He just wants you to tell others how He has changed your life. We may not always share our faith tactfully or with just the right words. God doesn't call us to do things perfectly. But He does call us to be obedient. Let's strive to make sharing our faith a regular part of our life.

LESSON FORTY-TWO

Change in Defense Proves Revolutionary

In 1993, Nebraska's defensive coaches changed a long-time philosophical approach in their front-seven player alignment. The retooling scheme would prove to be revolutionary en route to contending for the national title four times over a five-year period. After suffering through seven consecutive bowl losses, the staff recruited and implemented speed into the new attack-oriented defense. The switch to four down linemen and three linebackers revamped the old 5-2 read-and-react look of several years.

The high-flying attack style defense was a custom fit for All-American outside line-backers Trev Alberts, Jared Tomich, and Grant Wistrom.

Entering the defense's season debut, Alberts stated his thoughts on the new-look attack: "We have big expectations."

And it came as no surprise as the talented Alberts, the 1993 Butkus Award winner, pounded opposing quarterbacks with 15 sacks for minus 88 yards as he recorded 96 tackles that season. Yes, definitely give most of the credit to great athletes, coaching, preparation, and execution, but the new attacking scheme was truly pivotal to Nebraska's success in the 1990s.

The dramatic change in Nebraska's defense, though not original to the game of football, was birthed from simple X's and O's on a coach's chalk board. Who could have foreseen how big a role it would play in the winning of games and championships?

But far more impacting than that conceptual birth from the chalk board was the quiet birth of a Jewish baby two thousand years ago—that baby being God the Son, Jesus Christ. We celebrate His birth each Christmas, although the importance of it often gets lost in the busyness of the season. The Bible says, "The Word became flesh and made His dwelling among us" (John 1:14).

God entered this world as a baby. He was born in a quiet stable that no doubt smelled from the animals. The floor would have been hard and dirty. Could anyone have dreamed that the God of the universe would make such a quiet and lowly entry into the world? I'm sure a lot of people never knew the Savior of the world was born that night. Not because they were doing bad things, but because they weren't looking. Some things haven't changed in two thousand years.

How about you? Are you looking for the Savior? Do you understand how the world has been quietly changed by a little baby born two thousand years ago? Have you noticed how His birth has forever changed the course of history? Do you understand the significance of the most important event in history? The Master Inventor provided mankind with a way to salvation: Jesus Christ. Are you too busy to notice the most important event in your life and mine? Maybe it's time you looked beyond the creation and to the Creator. Don't forget to thank God for inventing a way to save us from ourselves.

LESSON FORTY-THREE

Player Attends Chapel Hoping For 'Good Luck'

It's not uncommon for superstitions to abound within the world of sports. An athlete may wear the same pair of socks unwashed game after game if he had great success the first time he wore them. At many universities, it's not unusual for football players to touch a horseshoe that hangs over the doorway as they head onto the field. Sadly, some people even pray before and after games for good luck. Former Nebraska wingback Clester Johnson admitted that prior to accepting Christ he attended game day chapels in hopes that it would enhance his team's on-field success.

"Every time I went to chapel, we won. It was good luck."

People may do the strangest things in hopes of having good luck. Nevertheless, God is not impressed with that misdirected faith. But how about you? Do you have a few superstitions?

I have to confess, I wore my midget football jersey all the way into high school. Not over my pads, you understand, but under them. The jersey, number 66, was my lucky charm. I bought it because my football hero wore the same number. I thought, just maybe, some of his skill, talent, luck, or whatever might just rub off on me.

It's an interesting thing about that old torn-up jersey. When I played college football my freshman year, the jersey mysteriously disappeared. I still suspect someone in my family. However, one of my teammates might have been sick of seeing and smelling the thing. But you know what? I didn't play any differently without it. I can't say I was really surprised. After all, I didn't really believe it helped. Or did I?

More often than not, our little superstitions become stumbling blocks to us, rules that somehow we've made up or believe affect the way we live. The same thing can happen in our spiritual lives. It's easy to let man-made rules replace God-made guidelines for living the Christian life.

Remember the time Jesus healed the man by the pool in John chapter 5? The man had been an invalid for thirty-eight years. Jesus healed him, but the religious leaders were upset because their picky laws forbade it.

What kind of man-made rules or superstitions do you believe about the Christian faith? Does length of hair or dress make someone less spiritual? Do you play and compete better simply because you pray? Do you use prayer like a rabbit's foot?

Superstition does one thing: It binds you. It enslaves you to a set of rules that makes life miserable. Especially when you create man-made rules for living your faith. Break the chains of superstitions and man-made rules. Never forget that Jesus Christ can liberate you. "Then you will know the truth, and the truth will set you free" (John 8:32).

LESSON FORTY-FOUR

Reception...
Out of Bounds

In any sport, officials make bad calls. Usually they are unintentional mistakes and just a part of the expected human imperfectness of the game. On Sept. 25, 1982, No. 2 Nebraska's 27-24 loss to eventual national champion Penn State at Beaver Stadium has been remembered by two key controversial plays during the game-winning drive.

On second and four at the Nebraska 17 with short seconds remaining, Penn State quarterback Todd Blackledge hit receiver Mike McCloskey for 15 yards. Taped replays indicate the ball was caught out of bounds. The following play, Blackledge's low two-yard pass to receiver Kirk Bowman was ruled complete in the end zone with four seconds on the clock. Replays show the ball may have been trapped on the game-winning touchdown pass.

"It was a complete drop," said former Cornhusker split end Todd Brown. "It wasn't even close enough to be a trap. The play that was worse than that was the play where the ball was caught out of bounds. I could see it—but we couldn't whine about it."

Fair or unfair, there's a good case that both plays were blown no-calls by the officials. Not to be critical, but those are the breaks, sometimes. Whether it was an honest mistake or not, sometimes the referee doesn't always see the play accurately. Speaking of not seeing something clearly, I can't help but think of all the times Jesus talked about spiritual blindness. In fact, the New Testament is full of references about spiritual blindness.

Jesus often used something everyone understood, like blindness, to make a point about the spiritual life.

When the disciples told Jesus that the religious leaders were offended by some of the things He said, Jesus responded by saying, "Leave them, they are blind guides. If a blind man leads a blind man, both will fall into a pit" (Matthew 15:14).

Jesus was making it clear to the disciples that they needed to leave the religious leaders alone. Just ignore them. They were blind to the truth. Anyone who listened to them risked spiritual blindness.

Today some religious leaders claiming to have a lock on truth lack spiritual eyesight. I'm not necessarily talking about the pastor at your church. I have in mind all the cults that have sprung up in America during the past decade. It's great to live in a country that allows religious freedom. But with freedom comes responsibility. You and I have a responsibility to make sure that the religious leaders we listen to follow the principles in Scripture.

Maybe you're not too concerned about the cults because you don't see their impact in your neighborhood. But look out! The one thing these spiritually blind guides count on is ignorance. They feed on the sheep that wander mindlessly into their fold.

Don't overreact to cults and false teachers by organizing a witch hunt. But don't fall into the other extreme of ignorance and complacency. God wants you to know the enemy. Don't go through life with a spiritual blindfold on. I'll close with a warning from the Bible. "Be very careful, then, how you live, not as unwise but as wise" (Ephesians 5:15).

LESSON FORTY-FIVE

Huskers Unite Against Kansas State

During Nebraska's 1994 national championship campaign, teamwork defined NU's resolve against Kansas State. The Cornhusker defense, offensive line, and running back Lawrence Phillips were heavily relied upon as the top two quarterbacks, Tommie Frazier and Brook Berringer, were sidelined with injuries. Frazier was said to be out for the season with a blood clot behind his right knee. Berringer suffered a partially collapsed lung against Oklahoma State, but would eventually see limited action while wearing a protective flak jacket. Thus, the able-bodied backup, Matt Turman, was given the starting nod for that game.

The injuries, coupled with wet weather, would limit Nebraska to a one-dimensional running assault. It was a drizzly mid-October in Manhattan, Kansas, and the 11th-ranked Wildcats were smelling a potential upset. Nebraska clung to a one-point lead for two quarters before clinching a 17-6 hard-fought victory. The Cornhusker defense limited the Cats to six points as cornerback Barron Miles set a school record with six pass breakups and NU linebacker Troy Dumas blocked an extra-point kick. Nebraska's football team played wounded, but it played together. And it played tough.

Almost any sport involves teamwork, putting together the different individual talents and blending them so they can accomplish more than they could on their own. A team that works together can accomplish much more than the separate members working individually.

It shouldn't surprise us to find out that God has a lot to say about teamwork. After all, even the Trinity—God, Jesus, and the Holy Spirit—are a blend of three different parts that become more than the sum of its parts.

One of my favorite verses on teamwork is Ecclesiastes 4:9, "Two are better than one because they have a good return for their labor." This verse teaches that it makes sense to work together. We can accomplish more as a team than by ourselves. We need to trust others and be a team member. It's better to have someone alongside in life than to go it alone.

First Corinthians says, "you are a temple of the Holy Spirit." The word "you" is plural. In other words, together we are the temple of the Holy Spirit. Together we glorify God. It doesn't matter what sport you play, teamwork doesn't work unless you help to make it work. We all need to relate and respond to each other. You see, someone needs you, and you need someone. You don't have to play football to understand that teamwork is like two minor tributaries of water joining to create a mighty river. Each of us needs to do his/her part to link up with others and form one balanced pool.

LESSON FORTY-SIX

Some Fans Hide Prejudice Until After the Game

In society, people may sometimes feel uncomfortable when they see people of differing races teaming up. Sadly, Sunday morning worship has become the most segregated time of the week for many Christians in America. Nebraska receivers' coach Ron Brown illustrated how sports fans who harbor traces of racial prejudice will cheer loudly for different races at a sporting event.

"I remember the 1997 Nebraska versus Oklahoma game in Memorial Stadium," Brown recalled. "Scott Frost, our quarterback, dropped back to pass. He looked down the field, and he saw a freshman sensation named Bobby Newcombe sprinting down the right hash mark. He lined a bullet pass to him that Bobby caught and sprinted into the end zone for a 48-yard touchdown.

"And do you think that at that moment 76,000 people in Memorial Stadium scratched their heads and said, 'Wow, that was white guy from Wood River, Neb., who just threw the ball to that black kid from Albuquerque, NM.' Ha! No. Seventy-six thousand fans across that stadium, as well as ranchers and farmers on their tractors and horses who could not make that game but were listening to the radio, stood to their feet like trained bears and all screamed, 'Touchdown! Yeah, great!'

"The question is, what happens when the players leave the field? Why do we cheer for that kind of teamwork on the field, but boo at that kind of teamwork when people of different races get together off the field? Seems to me that we could learn something from our athletes."

Some people in America think bigotry and racism have been overcome. But the image described by Coach Brown remains all too accurate for many people. Most white people don't run around wearing white robes and burning crosses. But many white people might tell a joke and not even realize how it makes someone of another race feel.

In sports, somebody always seems to be talking or writing about the differences between the races. It's not uncommon to hear comments like "He's sure fast for a white guy" or whatever the comparison for a particular race may be.

The Bible has a lot to say about how God looks at the differences between races. His perspective has never changed. "God does not show favoritism" (Romans 2:11).

Some of us have seen firsthand the problems with the hatred of bigotry and racism. Most of us have seen insensitivity and lack of understanding between the races. In fact, I doubt if any of us are totally without some prejudices. The cure for these problems is that each of us respond in obedience to God's Word. We need to love one another, just as Jesus did.

Jesus met a Samaritan woman at a well and loved her enough to change her life. Some of you, I'm sure, know the story. Maybe what you've missed is how He overlooked the fact that she was from a race of people that He shouldn't even have talked to, much less helped. But He did.

It takes understanding, love, concern, and a heart to do what God would do to overcome problems between races. As Christians, we need to do more than just give lip service to changing the way people treat each other. Each of us has a responsibility to speak out when favoritism or unfairness is shown because of race. And that's no joke.

Husker Not Afraid of Label

Husker running back Dan Alexander has demonstrated that he's not afraid to take a stand for Christ.

"I have a little dog tag that says, 'Jesus Freak,' " said the hulking, six-foot 250-pounder as he displayed the chain around his neck. "No one has ever called me a 'Jesus Freak,' but I wish they would. I think that's the biggest compliment we could receive. And I'm not afraid to wear this.

"Some people have called me 'freak' just because I'm big or something," Alexander chuckled. "But I'm not just a freak, I'm a Jesus freak."

The cheerful, soft-spoken Dan Alexander could frequently be found sporting Fellowship of Christian Athletes garb and other Christian T-shirts. But he preferred to let his actions speak for themselves.

"There's only so much you can do on a team of 160 guys, but your actions speak a lot louder than your words. It's one of those things where the younger guys come in, and you show them that you can have a good time without having to go to all the parties and drink all the booze and get all the girls. If people ask if I want to hang out, I'll say, 'Well, do you want to go to a movie or do something constructive—something that won't get us into trouble?'

"I realize that God is judging me all the time, so I want to be the best person I can be. And I have to be a witness to others. I have to help other people. So I like to help the younger players, not only to be better football players, but to be good people. I try to help them with their studies and keep them away from bad things. You can't preach to people because a lot of times it turns people off, so you have to lead by example. And then when people come and ask you about your faith or why you're different, then you can talk to them."

Someone compared a speed skier's descent down the first third of the slope, built at a 76-degree angle, to falling off a cliff. No doubt, those competitors have an extraordinary amount of ambition and courage. The life of a Christian can require just as much boldness, nerves, and guts. In fact, it takes all three of these qualities to resist negative peer pressure. Listen to the warning God gives in 1 Corinthians 15:33: "Do not be deceived, 'Bad company corrupts good morals,' " (v. 33) *The Living Bible* puts it this way: "Don't be fooled by those who say such things. If you listen to them, you will start acting like them."

In other words, if we spend enough time around the wrong people, our actions become like theirs. That's really common sense, isn't it? We would all like to think that we would be a greater influence on the people we're around than they would be on us. But often, their actions rub off more on us, don't they?

It takes boldness, nerves, and guts to think for yourself, resist the crowd influence, and take a stand for Jesus Christ. Don't forget, you're never really alone. After all, God said He would never leave or forsake you. So my advice is: Don't let others pressure you into doing things in order to be accepted by them. Instead, speak up for your own beliefs and follow God's standards in the Bible.

Frazier Storms Back

Nebraska quarterback Tommie Frazier had been held out during the majority of the 1994 national championship season with blood clots and did not see any action until he was given the starting nod in the Jan. 1, 1995, Orange Bowl against Miami. During the opening quarter, the Husker offense either stalled or turned the ball over. If fans had not already been wondering if Frazier's absence of playing time had affected his game, they might have been thinking about it at this point. Trailing 10-0 early in the second period, Coach Osborne replaced Frazier with Brook Berringer. The Huskers gained confidence and momentum behind Berringer's leadership and cut the margin to 17-9. Osborne reinstalled Frazier in the fourth quarter. And with 7:15 left, NU fullback Cory Schlesinger ran up the middle for the game-tying touchdown. Nebraska's physical play was taking its toll on the Hurricanes. About a minute later, the Huskers began their game-winning drive. Facing third and four at midfield, a healthy Frazier rushed 25 yards to the Miami 27. After being tackled, a jubilant Tommie Frazier leaped from the grassy turf, ecstatically spinning in the air. "Tommie's back!" Nebraska fans likely exclaimed throughout the stadium and the nation. The Cornhuskers scored the winning touchdown with 2:46 on the clock, and Frazier earned his second-straight Orange Bowl MVP award.

When Frazier scrambled for that first down late in the fourth quarter of the Orange Bowl, NU fans had little doubt that the 1994 preseason All-America candidate was back at full speed. Fans cheered with ecstasy along with him. Surpassingly greater, Christians should have an eagerness about the return of Jesus Christ. If we can get excited about the return of a football player, how much more should we be excited about the return of Jesus!

Christ's future return is known as the Second Coming. It's the most important future event that will take place. No one knows when it will happen . . . maybe soon. Sadly, a lot of people never give it a second thought. Others think it's a waste of time to focus on the Lord coming back.

But the Bible commands us to live in hope and expectation of His return. Titus 2:13 says, "Looking for the blessed hope and the appearing of our great God and Savior, Christ Jesus."

If you read God's Word, you will also find that His return is no minor issue. In fact, one out of every 30 verses in the Bible mentions the return of Christ or the end of time. Only four out of 27 New Testament books don't mention Christ's return.

Okay, so maybe you agree that it's important to think about His return, but so what? What difference should it make in our lives? A lot of people have misunderstood how to apply this verse to their lives. It doesn't teach us to go out and set dates for His return, or that we should quit school or our job and wait for His return on a roof top. It does mean we should live every day as if it's our last.

Now, please don't go out and cancel all your plans for the next few years. Plan like you'll be around for tomorrow, but live your life like He's coming back today.

While Christians might disagree on when He's coming back, one thing's for sure: He will return. Are you ready?

LESSON FORTY-NINE

Huskers Chart Course for Title

The Huskers finished the 1969 season at 9-2, ranked eleventh by the Associated Press. It was Nebraska's best record since 1966, after going 6-4 two straight seasons. Former Husker All-American offensive lineman Bob Newton said many media representatives touted Nebraska as one of the top three teams in the country, despite their final ranking.

Going into the next season, Husker players grew hungry for something unprecedented at their school—a national championship.

Bob Newton recalled, "We went into training camp in 1970 to go for a national championship. We felt that strong about our team.

"We really had the concept of a team. Everyone cared about one another and would sacrifice for their teammates. Today I see a lot of individualism in sports. I really felt that we represented the definition of 'team' that year."

The 1970 Huskers finished the regular season undefeated and went into the Orange Bowl ranked third behind Texas and Ohio State. But upsets to the Longhorns and Buckeyes on New

Year's Day set up an opportunity for Nebraska to play No. 5 Louisiana State for the national title.

And with 6:10 remaining in the fourth quarter of the Orange Bowl, the Huskers would seize that opportunity.

"In that drive, everything, the national championship, was on the line," recalled Newton. "And we had to get the ball in there and just give it 130 percent on every play and block our hearts out. I believe that the offense got that ball in there because they played with their hearts. Our heart was in that drive. Our whole season was hanging on this fourth quarter against LSU, and we had to get the job done."

It was third down, and the end zone was 36 inches away. NU quarterback Jerry Tagge kept the ball and dove over the middle of the pile. Tagge stretched across the goal line for the score as Nebraska went up 17-12.

The Cornhusker defense held the remainder of the match as the squad attained its hard-sought goal of a national championship.

A goal gives us a target to shoot at. A goal focuses our minds on the task, rather than the distractions. Does God care about our goals? Is He interested in the goals we set? Good questions. Let's take a moment to answer them. God cares about our goals because He cares about us and what we desire to accomplish. Goals help to determine who we are and what we do. For example: Moses' goal in the Bible was to follow God anywhere and gather people around him who would walk by faith. As a result, he rescued the Jews and led them toward the Promised Land.

Although you may set many goals, there is one ultimate goal each of us should strive toward: to glorify God. Here is a verse that lays the foundation for the ultimate goal:

"For you have been bought with a price; therefore, glorify God in your body" (1 Corinthians 6:20).

Setting goals to win championships, set records, and win games is fine, but glorifying God should be our ultimate goal. What exactly does glorifying God mean?

We glorify God when we draw attention to Him, not ourselves. We glorify God when we reflect His character and actions. Finally, we glorify God when we cause others to have a good opinion of Him because of the way we live our lives.

I challenge you: Set goals! Work toward your goals! Make your ultimate goal to glorify God!

LESSON FIFTY

'Emotional Whiplash' During Loss

The 1986 Huskers were 0-and-2 against the rival Oklahoma Sooners in the past two meetings and were sniffing a chance to get a piece of the Big Eight title. Ranked fifth in the country and 9-1 on the season, the emotionally charged Cornhuskers donned all-red uniforms for the first time to help psyche themselves up.

Nebraska scored midway through the first quarter and took a 17-7 lead into the final period. Confidence and high emotions raged through Husker players. But after trailing most of the afternoon, Oklahoma scored 13 points in the fourth quarter. Ten of those points came in the game's closing 90 seconds as No. 3 Oklahoma went on to a 20-17 win and secured a berth in the Orange Bowl.

With 1:22 remaining, Sooner All-American tight end Keith Jackson scored on a 17-yard touchdown pass from Jamelle Holieway to tie the game at 17. And with nine seconds on the clock, Jackson snagged a dramatic 41-yard pass on third down to set up a 31-yard game winning field goal by Tim Lasher.

"I was in shock," said former NU offensive captain Stan Parker as he recalled Lasher's kick through the uprights. "Before the last two minutes, I was emotionally high. To see that taken away in two minutes, I got emotional whiplash. I was just kind of numb."

Temporarily deflated, Husker players would have to wait until next season for a crack at their biggest rival and the conference title.

Almost every athlete has dreamed of winning a championship, a medal, or something they've put their heart into achieving. More often than not something happens, and suddenly, they know that they will never realize their dream.

Each of us faces different disappointments. One thing is common: It's painful to lose anything we work toward achieving. Most of us put a lot of time and energy into our dreams, don't we? Maybe you've just been cut from the varsity or made an error that cost you the big game. Maybe you're facing the ultimate disappointment of not being able to reach your ultimate long-term goal.

So the question becomes, "How do I forget about a disappointment and get on with my life?"

The apostle Paul found the answer and lets us in on it in Philippians 3:13-14, "Brethren, I do not regard myself as having laid hold of it [sinless perfection] yet, but one thing I do: Forgetting what lies behind and reaching forward to what lies ahead, I press toward the goal [to be Christlike] for the prize of the upward call of God in Christ Jesus."

It's only normal to let a negative experience influence our current action. That's why Paul tells us to leave our disappointments completely in the past. You see, Paul's ultimate goal was to be like Christ. There is no way to be 100 percent like Christ. So, rather than giving up on his goal, he put his mistakes behind him. Then he looked forward to the future.

You can do the same thing when something negative happens to you. Your mind can only focus 100 percent of its capacity on one thing at a time. The more you concentrate on letting the Holy Spirit help you be like Christ, the less influence the past disappointment will have on you.

The key is to focus so much on the goal of becoming like Christ in all you do that your failures become secondary. If you dream only of records, trophies, and prestige, you'll eventually be disappointed. But if you keep your focus on Christ, forget the past, then look forward to the future, you'll be able to play beyond even the worst disappointments.

LESSON FIFTY-ONE

Fryar Found Life Meaningless

On the outside, former Husker wingback Irving Fryar had every reason to be happy. He was a top receiver in the NFL, he was an All-American in college, and he was the No. 1 NFL draft pick in 1983. He was wealthy and famous. Yet, he was miserable to the point of wanting to kill himself. Fryar explained how empty he was because he needed the Lord in his life.

"There were a lot of things that kept me separated from Christ when I was in the world. I began to make some wrong decisions. I got involved in drugs. I started hanging around with the wrong people, going to the wrong places, doing the wrong things. Things were pretty bad, so I started to hibernate. I started not caring about people and not caring about myself. There was a time when I even tried to take my own life."

But Irving did repent and prayed to accept Jesus Christ as his Savior and Lord. He realized how vain life truly is without a relationship with God through Christ.

"All the awards, all of the accolades, all of the nice things that people say to me, all of the TV, all of the money, all of that stuff doesn't amount to a hill of beans without knowing Jesus Christ."

Though Irving Fryar received great wealth and acclamation as a star NFL and collegiate athlete, he was empty before he found the Lord. And tragically, similar thoughts of suicide are becoming more common in our society. It doesn't just affect athletes, but also millions of teen-agers who are trying to deal with life. Each day in the United States, over seventy people commit suicide.

Athletes often feel like they are placed in a fishbowl for everyone to watch. If you fail, everyone sees you lose. If you make a mistake, everyone sees it. While athletes put pressure on themselves, sometimes parents, friends, and family add to it. Sometimes the pressure to perform closes in like a vise. Athletes often don't see any way to get away from the pressure that is making life seem unbearable.

Even the prophet Elijah in the Old Testament went through incredible emotional highs and lows. He felt deep stress as he fled from the wicked Queen Jezebel, who ordered him to be killed. In 1 Kings chapter 19, Elijah escaped into the wilderness and wished that he could die. But God comforted him and enabled him to accomplish His will. Just prior to his depression, 1 Kings chapter 18 explains how God had provided an incredible miracle before him. But when Elijah's life was threatened by the wicked queen, he felt he had endured enough. In his anguish, Elijah failed to realize how God was caring for him and was taking him through the difficult times. Nevertheless, the Lord continuously demonstrated His grace and provision.

God wants us to persevere when life gets hard. It's true, life is hard, but God is good. It's a fact of life. And God calls us to trust in Him through everything. We need to cling to Him in faith. We need to trust God even when life doesn't make sense.

In Romans 8:18, the Apostle Paul says, "For I consider that the sufferings of this present time are not worthy to be compared with the glory which shall be revealed in us."

Yes, the sufferings of the present can be incredibly painful and not make any sense, but God will take us through those times. He will give us His peace if we seek Him with our whole heart. We need to trust Him with our whole heart because He is faithful and His promises are true. Isaiah 26:3-4 says, "You will keep him in perfect peace, whose mind is stayed on You, because he trusts in You. Trust in the Lord forever, for in Jehovah, the Lord is everlasting strength."

I've found one particular Bible verse that has helped me overcome worry and frustration: "Trust in the Lord with all your heart, and do not lean on your own understanding. In all your ways acknowledge Him, and He will make your paths straight" (Proverbs 3:5-6).

It's important to understand from this verse that you need to respond to the pressure by trusting God. In other words, it's your choice; nobody can do it for you. When you feel pressure building, take time to reflect on Proverbs 3:5-6. Then, totally trust God, not relying on your own perspective, and depend on Him for your strength and direction. I'm convinced that God wants you to be living proof, showing how smart it is to commit your life to following His ways and trusting in Him. The solution to all our problems is Jesus Christ.

Virginity: Publicly Mocked, Privately Respected

In an age when chastity is publicly mocked, it is still secretly respected. Former Husker linebacker Aaron Penland has recalled times when teammates would question his commitment to remain a virgin until marriage.

"People asked why I am a virgin, and I just told them I'm a Christian," Penland noted. "That's just something you are supposed to save until you're married. A lot of them laughed, but then they eventually came to respect me.

"One time when I went to some charity senior basketball games, my teammates started talking about girls and the subject came up that I was a virgin. Some of them said that if they had to do it over again that they would [remain a virgin].

"I have had a girlfriend for three years now, and it's getting more and more difficult," he explained. "There are times when things can get out of hand in a hurry if you don't watch yourself. You don't know who you are going to marry. If you are dating a girl, you need to respect her. You might think you are going to end up with her, but if you take that girl's virginity, you can spoil it for her.

"God has the perfect mate out there for you. And if you just wait, in His time, He will make it come about."

Penland stressed that the potential for contracting sexually transmitted diseases should be a strong reason in itself to remain abstinent.

"There's no telling what you can get. A lot of these guys are just loading a gun and putting it to their head. Sometimes they don't even know the person [they sleep with], and there's no telling what they've got. How is that going to impact you 10 years down the road when you find that you've gotten something?"

Hebrews 13:4 says, "Marriage should be honored by all, and the marriage bed kept pure, for God will judge the adulterer and all the sexually immoral."

Scripture makes it clear that sexual relations are to be reserved solely for marriage. It seems redundant to explain how sex is constantly promoted in society. Sadly, the world has attempted to reduce it to a simple act that gives pleasure whenever someone chooses. People would like to believe that it is no more harmful than eating too many sweets and that you just have to be careful not to get burned. Sex is a gift from God designed solely for marriage between one man and one woman as God ordained for husband and wife to "become one flesh" (Genesis 2:20b-24). And as sex is designed for husband and wife, it is not for man and man or woman and woman. Leviticus 18:22 and Romans 1:26-27 explain how homosexuality is abominable before God.

In 1 Corinthians 6:18-20, the apostle Paul explains how we need to run from sexual temptation and not sin against our own body:

"Flee from sexual immorality. All other sins a man commits are outside his body, but he who sins sexually sins against his own body...Therefore, honor God with your body."

People often tend to view a sexual relationship as something that can be without consequence as long as no one gets pregnant or picks up a sexually transmitted disease. They view the sexual relationship as if it were like velcro. Velcro can be attached and pulled apart with none to minimal wear. But sex is more like super glue. Imagine two pieces of wood super-glued together. In a sexual relationship, there is a deep emotional and physical bond that was designed to be permanent. So what happens when you attempt to pull the two pieces of wood apart? Well, they don't easily come apart, and there is no clean break. Both pieces will end up with splinters and pieces of the other wood still attached. That bonding was not meant to be broken. And as the wood is damaged, the pain of a sexual relationship outside marriage can last a lifetime. No moment of pleasure is worth that pain, not to mention that it also is displeasing to God.

Sex was created to reproduce life. Anyone who has sex outside of marriage is literally taking someone else's life and future into his/her hands. But someone may say, "But I love her" or "I love him." In reality, true love waits and respects. It wants God's best for the other person. It is not selfish.

And don't fall for the "safe sex" myth. Nothing prevents pregnancies or sexually transmitted diseases 100 percent of the time. Don't play Russian roulette with your life and someone else's. The only safe sex is with a wedding ring.

But what if you have already had sexual relations outside marriage? Have you confessed it to God and repented? If you have genuinely told God you are sorry and have asked for forgiveness, know that He has forgiven you. God loves you deeply and wants to help you with your burden. And meanwhile, remain abstinent until marriage. God will honor your commitment to obedient living.

Remember that sex is a gift from God and was created with a price tag called integrity, self-discipline, and responsibility before God. And that gift can only be received in the confines of marriage.

LESSON FIFTY-THREE

Friendship Permeates Team

The pair of 6-foot-5 towering All-American defensive linemen were inseparable like brothers. Lombardi Trophy-winning rush end Grant Wistrom of Webb City, Mo., and defensive tackle Jason Peter of Locust, N.J., ripped apart opposing offensive lines together during their three-year starting career that spanned the 1995 and 1997 national championship campaigns.

As senior defensive co-captains in 1997, the high-spirited teammates combined for 15.5 sacks and 32 tackles for losses. Best friends and roommates, they even left college football together in the first round of the NFL draft.

The two giants shared many light-hearted moments together. Following their final spring game, Peter jokingly chided Wistrom that he had better have dinner ready for him when he got home.

Not only their talent, but their consistent vigor and leadership were crucial as Nebraska chased the 1997 national title. Their spirit of unity and commitment transcended upon and symbolized that year's football team.

Grant Wistrom and Jason Peter's genuine brotherhood demonstrated the positive difference friendships can make. The two not only excelled by pushing each other, but their spirit of teamwork permeated through the whole team. We need other people. The Bible says, "Two are better than one because they have a good return for their labor. For if either of them falls, the one will lift up his companion. But woe to the one who falls when there is not another to lift him up" (Ecclesiastes 4:9-10).

True friendships are needed, but rarely happen on their own. An interesting verse in the Bible on friendships is found in Proverbs 18:24. "A man of many friends comes to ruin, but there is a friend who sticks closer than a brother." The word "ruin" literally means "to be shaken so violently that you fall to pieces."

In other words, the Bible is teaching that we need a few close friends that we can count on. If we can't find those friends, we won't have the support we need. Many friendships are broad, but not deep. We all need to build friendships that have depth to them.

How do you build this type of friendship? First, be open to the other person. It's impossible to develop a solid friendship without being open and honest about yourself and others. Second, develop an attitude of acceptance. We all need to feel loved and accepted. No friendship can survive without this kind of attitude.

Now let me ask you: Do you have friendships that are based on openness and acceptance? If not, it's time to start. Pray that God will put godly Christian friends in your life. And above all, pray that He will help you to be a godly friend to those around you. This week . . . yes, this week, when you get together with your teammates to work out, start to develop friendships that are based on honesty and acceptance.

Homosexuals Need to be Shown Christ's Love

The following commentary by Nebraska receivers' coach Ron Brown is from a radio broadcast: "Why did the chicken cross the road? Give up? The answer is, because he was chicken. In the parable of the Good Samaritan, this familiar story points to a strange phenomenon that is so prevalent in our time. The priest and Levite both saw a man who was beaten and half dead. It's bad enough that they wanted no part in helping this guy. But why did they take the time to cross the road? Do we fear what we see? You don't have to deal with what you don't see, do you? Fear causes strange reactions.

"A few boys at my grade school and in my neighborhood seemed to be more effeminate than one would think they should. We wrongfully called them sissies and attacked these boys without mercy. Often during school recess, a group of us would pounce upon such a boy, smashing the poor kid's face into the sand and tearing his clothes. I knew nothing about homosexuality in grade school. But I sensed these so-called sissies as being threatening in some way to me.

"But it didn't stop there. While in college in the 1970s, when the gay community began to openly take its sinful behavior to the public square, my athletic buddies and I plotted to discredit them. I have to admit, my hatred for them didn't end after I became a Christian at the end of my college years. The hate didn't plot for violence, but I still viewed them as the enemy.

"After trusting Christ, I sensed change in each area of my life, except in my outlook on the homosexual. Believe me, I have a huge heart for evangelism, exhortation, and mercy for those lost in sin without Christ. I have often responded to God's call face to face with those in need of Christ's love, except the homosexual. Oh, I want to see them evangelized, exhorted, and shown mercy, but from a distance. They were God's worst enemies, as far as I was concerned. There's no question that homosexuality is clearly wrong, according to God's Word."

Ron Brown continued by stating, "Jesus went to the cross for the homosexual, just as He did for everyone else. The Good Samaritan didn't cross the street; he ministered personal love and attention to the hurting man. Today, it seems like the Christian and the homosexual hate each other. Too many of us Christians are crossing the road. We have left the homosexual on the side of the road, beaten and hurting, to a politically correct world that honors this lifestyle; that has evangelized them into a lost existence; that exhorts them with their liberal religious clergy; and that provides mercy to them from its government in the form of dollars, media time, and accepted entry into school curriculums. The homosexual is both lost and beaten up, despite his politically strong appearance, and needs the love of Jesus.

"But the people of Jesus have abandoned them. In all of my years of formerly physically and verbally thrashing the homosexual, I have yet to see one of them beaten into heterosexuality. The boy 'sissies' of yesteryear that I physically abused have grown up to be overt homosexuals, as have the young college gays. They are now men; some with AIDS, all lost without Christ. Fear and hate won't do it, Christian! The homosexual is part of Jesus' Great Commission. It's going to take the up-close, intimate love of Jesus through you and me to win the homosexual to Christ. And isn't that what it's all about, ultimately? And it will be Christ who will show them what the real lifestyle is supposed to be.

"First John 4:18 says, 'There is no fear in love. But perfect love drives out fear, because fear has to do with punishment. The one who fears is not made perfect in love.' I am convicted and repentant," said Coach Brown.

With the rising prevalence of homosexuality and push for gay rights in society, Coach Brown's message is critical. His words also raise several important questions. First, is homosexuality a sin? Second, should Christians take a stand for moral values in our society, regardless of the pressure put on them personally? Third, should a particular lifestyle receive certain protections from society? Fourth, if you oppose homosexuality, are you a hate monger or homophobic? There was a time in our society when nobody wanted to talk about homosexuality. Now you can't miss the moral battles on TV. If it's not a dispute over some piece of art being funded by the National Endowment of the Arts, it's a protest in New York by gay people who want to be included in the St. Patrick's Day march.

Is homosexuality a sin? There are several places in the Old Testament where homosexuality is condemned as sin. Leviticus 18:22 says, "Do not lie with a man as one lies with a woman; that is detestable."

It's true that Jesus didn't specifically talk about this sin. It just wasn't a problem among the Jews. The Apostle Paul did talk about it because it was a common problem in the Greco-Roman culture he ministered to. Although Jesus didn't speak about homosexuality, He did talk about human sexuality. Whenever He spoke on an issue like divorce, it was assumed He was coming from a heterosexual position because He always pointed back to the Creation for the basis of His arguments.

The apostle Paul gives us the most specific verse in the New Testament on homosexuality. Romans 1:26, 27 say, "Because of this, God gave them over to shameful lusts. Even their women exchanged natural relations for unnatural ones. In the same way the men also abandoned natural relations with women and were inflamed with lust for one another. Men committed indecent acts with other men, and received in themselves the due penalty for their perversion." Here Paul condemns the actions of both lesbians and male homosexuals. He said that both men and women exchanged their natural relations for unnatural ones. We see that God didn't inspire anyone to become homosexual.

Many churches today have adopted society's stand on this issue and not only accept, but actually promote homosexuals into leadership roles. Society should not set the standards for Christians. Just because homosexuals have considerable political clout, doesn't mean Christians should adopt society's current set of "politically-correct" standards.

We need to remind ourselves that as Christians, we have a responsibility to take a stand for moral issues today, but we also need to recognize that God is willing to accept anyone who is willing to come to Him in faith. We as Christians need to respond to the homosexual with Christ-like love. We cannot walk by fearfully and think that it's someone else's responsibility to show them God's love. We need to love the sinner and hate the sin.

Confident 'Turmanator'

He was a 5'11", 165-pound walk-on backup quarterback, but he was appropriately nicknamed "The Turmanator." On October 15, 1994, at No. 16 Kansas State, the third-string Matt Turman became the first walk-on signal caller to start in nearly a decade. With Tommie Frazier out with a blood clot and Berringer's status iffy with a partially collapsed lung, tremendous pressure hung over the Wahoo native. Many fans supported him, but held their breath hoping No. 1 Nebraska could hang on with the short walk-on at the controls.

A week prior, the sophomore took over the throttle against Oklahoma State in Lincoln with his team clinging to a second half 9-3 lead. Quarterback coach Turner Gill told the young man to relax and take a deep breath before he went to work against the Cowboys. The confident, yet non-boasting Turman directed the Huskers to a 32-3 win over OSU. Against the Wildcats, he helped NU to a 7-6 halftime lead until Berringer could grip the reins.

The Turmanator was competitive on the field. And though he finished his Husker career as a backup player, his cheerful demeanor was always a welcome presence.

"Matt had an excellent attitude," reflected receivers' coach Ron Brown. "Here's a guy who could have easily sought another position. When he first came here, he was a receiver to start with. Then switched to quarterback.

"There were always questions about Matt's ability: Was he big enough? Was he fast enough? Was he strong enough? Could he throw well enough? But the guy's heart and knack of somehow finding a way to get things done reflected the attitude that he had. He was a well-prepared athlete. He had a very coachable attitude. He had a very team-oriented attitude. And he was always ready to deliver the goods when called upon."

Matt Turman could have allowed his circumstances as a backup player and being considered too short by some to get him down. Rather, he focused on what he could do and chose to excel.

Mental blocks stare all athletes in the face. It doesn't matter if you run track or play golf. Sooner or later, something will appear impossible. After all, take the four-minute mile. At one time, it was thought to be a barrier that was unbreakable. For example, look at the long jump. When Bob Beamon set the world record, many so-called experts predicted that his record would never be broken. They said it just couldn't be done. But it was broken, wasn't it?

Do you have any mental blocks? Maybe you don't see how you can possibly break into the starting lineup. Maybe you don't think you can jump higher, run faster, or throw farther. Almost anything can become a mental block. And they aren't always found in sports. Some students think they can't achieve higher grades or get into college.

In the Bible, the greatest example of a man who refused to let anything or anyone be a barrier was Noah. You remember the story from Sunday School. Here was a man that God told to build a huge ark and fill it with two of every kind of animal. You can bet there were a lot of people who tried to tell him to stop. He refused to let anything get in his way of serving God.

Noah did what many thought was impossible. When Bob Beamon broke the world record, it seemed he had accomplished the impossible. When Roger Bannister broke the four-minute-mile barrier, it seemed like a miracle. Yet, each of these feats probably had more to do with removing the mental blocks than anything else.

Listen to what God says about removing barriers: "Because you have so little faith, I tell you the truth, if you have faith as small as a mustard seed, you can say to this mountain, 'Move from there to there' and it will move. Nothing will be impossible for you" (Matthew 17:20).

Now don't miss the point here. Jesus didn't mean this verse should be taken physically and literally. After all, most people don't need to remove a physical mountain. He meant that if you have enough faith, all problems or barriers can be solved, and even the hardest task can be accomplished.

I don't know if God wants you to break a world record or even the school record. I do know that He wants you to compete without mental blocks. As Yogi Berra might say, "Mental blocks only get in your way."

Get rid of the mental blocks in your life. Start to depend on God for what seems impossible or improbable. Just maybe, you'll be surprised by how much He can do through you!

Receiver Grows Into Servant-Leader

When Ron Brown joined the Husker football staff in 1987 to coach the receivers, a young wingback helped him to feel at home in his new surroundings. Unlike many football coaches who have served at the University of Nebraska, Brown had no prior connection to the Husker program. And though accepted by his peers and players, sophomore receiver Richard Bell helped bring him into the fold.

"When I first came to Nebraska, one of the guys who really wired to me in terms of loyalty and in terms of me being the new receivers' coach was Richard Bell. He was the first one to give me his stamp of approval and endorsement, that 'Coach, I'm going to follow you, I'm going to trust you, and I want to learn all I can from you.' And the beginning of that relationship was the foundation for not only his growth as a player, but my growth as a coach. It was also a benefit for our football team.

"Richard Bell became a vital cog in our football team. He was an example of what it meant to serve others. He did little things like handing out pencils during tests. He handed out towels on the field. Even after he became a starting player late in his sophomore year, I saw him taking young players under his wing. He spent hours going over things on the board with some of the younger players, even when we were having double practices and the guys were tired and just wanted to go to sleep.

"You talk about a full-circle relationship with a player. He came to me as the loyal servant-player, and I saw the leadership reproduced in his life so that he then became the servant-leader of a group of younger players. And then I watched him go on to play pro football and become a Christian. Now he's a policeman out in southern California. It's been great seeing him trust Jesus Christ and seeing how God tied that player-coach relationship together to go beyond just becoming a better player."

Richard Bell's servant-like role on the team and with Coach Brown was symbolic of a healthy parent-teen relationship and how that can filter out to others. Bell wasn't trying to be a "goody-two-shoes" and gain favoritism with Coach Brown. He was simply being available to help out. The conscientious player was concerned about being an encouragement and aid to his peers and those above him.

In the parent-teen relationship, most teens want to be independent from their parents. They want their own identity, to be their own person, and to make their own choices. Parents often view this attitude as rebellion. Teens see it as healthy and absolutely necessary. About the same time, the hormones kick in. It makes a confusing mess! Nobody is happy. Nobody is satisfied with the situation. Yet, life must go on.

How should parents and teens deal with this problem? The advice from the secular talk shows is shallow and empty. Advice from friends is seldom constructive. God has given us the answers in the Bible for both parents and teens.

Parents do have a responsibility to treat their children with respect. Sometimes that doesn't happen. It doesn't take the kids off the hook from obeying their parents. Remember, God has commanded children to obey their parents, even when they seem to be wrong. The first of the Ten Commandments that attaches a promise to a commandment says, "Honor your father and your mother so that you may live long in the land the Lord your God is giving you" (Exodus 20:12).

What does it mean to honor your parents? It means speaking positively about them and politely to them. It means showing them courtesy and respect. To not obey them is to disobey God. Believe it or not, most parents want the best for their children. They have invested a lot in them. They are usually concerned about their future. Parents may not be perfect, but they are the only parents most of us will ever have. God gave us parents, and we need to be thankful for them. The Ten Commandments are not suggestions.

Most teens may experience the rite of passage through teenage rebellion to some degree. However, every teen can choose to move beyond it. The teen years need not be a battle ground between parents and teens. Don't rationalize and say, "Well, that's just the way I am." Call it what it is, rebellion. And say, "Lord, I need your help." Only He can turn turmoil into understanding. Only He can smooth the rough waters that develop between teens and parents. Take my advice: Turn to the Lord. Do it now. You'll be glad you did it sooner than later.

Anger Hinders Receiver's Performance

It's been said that there is no "I" in the word "team." But playing with a spirit of unchecked anger can be at least as detrimental to a team's performance as self-centeredness. Nebraska receivers' coach Ron Brown recalled a talented receiver whose selfish anger handicapped his effectiveness on the field.

"He wanted the ball so bad in a particular game," Brown said. "And that was all he could think about. When things didn't go his way—whether it be with the play calling or something happening when a ball was going to come his way or someone making a mistake—he would get so furious. He did this in a couple games and took himself out of the game. In one particular game, he began to play his own game and tried to invent ways to get the ball. He got out of the context of the whole team. Thus, his game went downhill, even though we won the game. It was a disastrous day for him. He wouldn't put mistakes behind him and just go on with the next play. He didn't keep [his anger] in check; he'd just let it build up. It was a terrible night for him. As a coach when you see that, you take him out of the game because he can possibly be detrimental to other people."

Thomas Jefferson suggested a way to handle anger in his *Rules of Living*: "When angry, count ten before you speak; if very angry, a hundred." Later, Mark Twain jokingly modified it to: "When angry, count four. When very angry, swear."

The athlete that Coach Brown described above demonstrated how his temper not only ruined his own performance, but could have been detrimental to his teammates. If most of us are honest, we've struggled at times with controlling our anger. A bad temper can lose games, lose friends, and hurt our families. Anger needs to be talked about, understood, admitted, and kept under wraps, or it will damage much more than how we perform in sports.

Let's examine a key verse in Scripture on how to control anger in Ephesians 4:26, 27: "Be angry, and yet do not let the sun go down on your anger, and do not give the devil an opportunity to defeat you."

At first glance, it looks like God is saying, "Get mad!" And that's true, but don't miss what God is trying to teach in this verse: First, when is it right to get mad? Consider the behavior of Jesus Christ. Jesus Himself showed anger when He drove the money changers out of the temple. He later nailed the religious teachers to the wall with His words. The only time in Scripture where anger is okay is when God's Word or will is disobeyed. It's not okay to blow up for the wrong reasons or when things don't go our way.

Second, anger is an emotion, like love, that God has given you and me. There is nothing unusual about expressing either emotion. It is not necessarily any worse to get angry than to show love.

In this verse Paul gives us two things to watch carefully when we start to become angry. He warns us not to stay angry. When we do, we cannot allow the devil an opportunity to use our anger to serve his purposes, rather than God's.

Each of us needs to control our anger. You can either choose to control your temper with God's help, or you can choose to let it control you. Either way, the choice is yours.

LESSON FIFTY-EIGHT

Emptiness in Following the Wrong Crowd

Former Nebraska backup split end Aaron Davis has seen a lot. A walk-on from the 1992-94 seasons, A.D. allowed himself to be molded by negative peer influence. In the spring of 1995, Davis quit football. He saw his non-football friends seemingly enjoying life in the fast lane. Thus, he followed suit and fully delved into the world of sex, drugs, and alcohol. But Aaron was not fulfilled, even with a 1994 national championship.

"I quit playing in 1995 because of peer pressure," recalled Davis. "After we won the national championship, I was no longer fulfilled. I saw my peers having more fun than I was. So I allowed my non-football peers to influence me to do the things that they were doing—doing drugs, getting high, drinking heavily. I even contemplated suicide because it got so bad. There's consequences to falling to peer pressure.

"The turning point was October 17, 1995. I was mentally tired. Physically, it was like my body was decaying because of the sin that I was involved in. I knew that I was going to hell. No question about it. That scared me."

The son of a preacher, Davis said he knew the truth of the gospel all too well. Thus, in mid-October, Davis prayed to accept Christ's forgiveness upon his life.

A short time later, a tragic event prompted Davis to share the good news as a full-time evangelist.

"My roommate was murdered shortly after that in June," Davis said. "I don't think he was a believer. I had tried to share with him on a number of occasions. And he always thought he had time [to make a decision].

"My message is that time waits for nobody. Peer pressure is not worth eternal separation from Christ. Jobs, money, sports, national championships—those can't satisfy. They were not meant to satisfy. Only the love and grace of Jesus Christ can satisfy.

"I've tried everything else. Sex didn't make me happy. Marijuana couldn't do it. Alcohol fell short. National championship rings are nice, but they begin to rust. The Bible says not to store up your treasures in earthly things that will rust and corrode, but to store up grace and mercy, the riches that come from Jesus Christ."

Rather than make a positive impact upon his peers, Aaron Davis followed after the party scene of his friends. Aaron had been clearly taught the difference between right and wrong. And he obviously knew better than to closely associate with people who could drag him down. Fortunately, he came to his senses and chose to get right with God.

Jesus told His disciples in John 17 that they were to be "in" the world (vs. 11), but not "of" the world (vs. 16).

These verses teach that since we live in the world, we are involved with the world. How involved should we be? The New Testament clearly teaches that we need to be careful to not become entangled with it like Aaron Davis did.

When Jesus said His disciples were to be "in" the world, He meant they mixed with people who were their neighbors, but who may oppose God's system of values. They might live next door or be your teammates, but they may not share the same set of values. When Jesus told His disciples not to be "of" this world, He meant they were not to get their values from the world. Instead, they were to get their values from God's system. In other words, we are not to mingle with the world, but rather we are to witness to the world. Like Christ, we are to love the people in the world, but not their sins.

Here is where the rub lies: We must be able to associate with and love those in the world without being influenced or swayed by them. We need to keep from being contaminated by their values. We should be in the world, but the world should not be in us. It's okay for the ship to be in the sea, but it's bad when the sea gets into the ship.

Simply put, the Bible says, "Do not conform any longer to the pattern of this world, but be transformed by the renewing of your mind" (Romans 12:2). This doesn't just end with refusing to conform to certain behaviors and customs, but to also allow the Holy Spirit to redirect our minds.

In the final analysis, choose to follow God's set of values. There is no neutral ground when it comes to values. Don't mix your worlds up, or you may find yourself walking away from God's values.

LESSON FIFTY-NINE

Freedom From Lust

Aaron Wills, Cornhusker rush end of the late '90s, was admittedly a prisoner of his sinful desires until he found the Lord.

"Through high school [and up until recent years] I had developed a lot of bad habits. I had developed a drinking problem. I had used marijuana consistently through high school. As I got out of high school and into college, my habits got a lot worse. As I started partying through my first semesters in college, I was not able to attend the [Jan 2, 1996] Fiesta Bowl National Championship game because I had to attend a drug treatment program. After I finished that program, I flirted with disaster. And I call it flirting because I was straddling the fence. I started to learn about God, but I wouldn't let go of my past. I still used marijuana and drank off and on. I was still having sex outside of marriage."

But after failing a drug test and being suspended from the team, Aaron knew he needed to ask forgiveness and repent before God.

"I got down on my knees and I told the Lord, 'Lord, there's nothing in my life that I need more than you right now,'" Wills said. "And He saw my heart. And through that, ever since then, God has just been building me up and breaking me down and molding me into His creation."

Among other temptations, Aaron Wills was formerly enslaved by lust. But through forgiveness and a new life in Christ, he found the tools to victoriously battle those fleshly desires. Aaron explained how he hopes his testimony will point others away from falling into the same sinful lifestyle habits he was once enslaved to.

"God kept me for a specific reason so that I could share my testimony with other people so that they wouldn't do the same things and go through the things I went through."

The lifestyle of many athletes, pro or otherwise, can be risky business. Many place themselves in positions to become targets of sexual temptations. For them, the temptations are just too much. If you question the risk, ask Magic Johnson, who contracted HIV from his promiscuous lifestyle.

For some athletes, the role of playboy or athlete is one in the same. Wilt Chamberlain boasted of sleeping with thousands of women during his playing days. The playing around has little to do with romance for either partner.

The problem is lust. It's not a new problem. In the Bible, one of the strongest men, Samson, was dropped in his tracks by lust. Lust was the one enemy he couldn't beat. He was attracted to the opposite sex by outward appearance only, not unlike many athletes today. Samson, when lusting after a woman said, "Get her for me, for she looks good to me." A lot of athletes say or think that same thing about the opposite sex.

Lust is a problem because it affects everyone. It's impossible in our society to avoid the junk that pours into our homes through TV, movies, and music. These three areas of entertainment alone put many wrong desires in front of our eyes on a regular schedule.

So what's the solution? Unplug the TV? Boycott the movies? Burn the CD's? Not necessarily, but we obviously need be careful to avoid anything that could cause us to stumble and to guard our hearts and affections. We must use godly discretion. We need to realize that what we take in does impact us. But we cannot resist temptation without God's help. Many have tried and failed. There is only one way to beat lust.

"No temptation has seized you except what is common to man. And God is faithful; He will not let you be tempted beyond what you can bear. But when you are tempted, He will also provide a way out so that you can stand up under it" (1 Corinthians 10:13).

Let's get specific. First, you haven't been tempted to do anything that is new to mankind. Wrong desires or temptations happen to everyone. Second, others have beaten lust or temptations, and so can you. Third, follow the Bible's advice on beating temptation. Here's how: (1) Identify the people or situations that give you problems. (2) Get away from anything you know is wrong. (3) Decide to do what is right. (4) Pray for God's help and support yourself with friends who will help you resist temptation.

Don't mess with lust. The first look might be harmless. But eventually, you'll get burned. After all, you don't have to be an athlete for promiscuity to be risky business.

LESSON SIXTY

A Plea Against Pornography

During the early 1990s, an organization took a stance against pornography using billboards to promote the slogan, "Real Men Don't Use Porn." The announcements featured images of various well-known and respected Americans who aligned themselves with this cause. One of those "Real Men" selected was Nebraska coach Tom Osborne. In retrospect, Osborne talked about the harmful impact of pornography.

"I feel our whole culture is in some trouble in terms of what we dwell on," Osborne explained. "You think of the impact of television. Many young people are spending more than 50 hours a week watching television. Some of the music is really counter-cultural. Some of the movies are very violent. We've seen the effects of this. So, it seems to me, that it's very important that we dwell on, like [the apostle] Paul says [in Philippians 4:8], if anything is lovely, if anything is true, honorable, and so on. As a culture, we really have ceased to focus on those things which are uplifting, which are of God. And

we focus on things that are the opposite. So, it seems to me that pornography is a slippery slope that engulfs some people, and it's been very damaging to our young people. It's been very denigrating to women. I see nothing good coming out of it. And I think most people who are involved in violent crimes against women and children are people who are into pornography.

"The first amendment people will always tell you there's no relationship between what you read and what you see and how you act out. Well, if that's true, then why in the world do we spend billions of dollars on advertising every year? If what you read and see and experience doesn't influence behavior, then why in the world do these same organizations that rely on advertising dollars do the advertising?

"I think that pornography is very destructive. It's about a $10-billion industry. And who knows the amount of human suffering that it produces every year?"

Good call, Coach! But Tom Osborne has not been alone in this drive to stamp out pornography. More and more athletes and coaches are speaking out in the fight against pornography.

Anthony Munoz, one of the NFL's best offensive linemen, refused to have his picture taken by *Playboy* magazine when he was named to the collegiate All-American team. Later, in his pro career, *Playboy* called back to do a feature article on him as part of its preseason football issue. Again, Munoz turned them down. For more than two years, he has been a part of Cincinnati's Citizens Concerned for Community Values.

Pornography is big business; earning estimates range as high as $10 billion per year. Some estimates show that there are four times as many adult bookstores in the United States as there are McDonald's restaurants. And cable TV and "dial-a-porn" telephone services have made pornography even more accessible. While children and women are exploited in the name of free speech, the impact on those who use the pornography is impossible to measure.

Researchers may argue over the amount of influence pornography has on people, but one thing is clear. It does influence our behavior. If advertisers spend millions of dollars each year to influence our behavior to buy their goods, isn't it obvious that the images people see in pornographic magazines would leave their mark?

The Bible says, "For as a man thinks within himself, so he is" (Proverbs 23:7). The idea is we become what we think about. We're influenced by the images we put in our mind.

Viewing pornography can literally cheapen a person's thoughts and diminish his/her respect toward others. In effect, pornography can lead a man to view women as pieces of meat. As former Husker coach Tom Osborne mentioned, pornography has often been linked to violent crimes against women.

The Lord even addresses that looking lustfully upon a woman is a sin. In Matthew 5:28, Jesus said, "But I tell you that anyone who looks at a woman lustfully has already committed adultery with her in his heart."

So what can you do to take a stand against pornography? First, stay away from it. First Corinthians 6:18 says, "Flee from sexual immorality. All other sins a man commits are outside his own body, but he who sins sexually sins against his own body."

Second, speak out against it when given an opportunity. No game is won by one person. And pornography is a problem that needs the help of all of us. Whether you're an athlete or not, people value what you have to say. Don't be shy! Make the call. You can make a difference, but only if you take a stand.

LESSON SIXTY-ONE

Huskers Make Case For Title

Who's number one? Following the 1997 season, the stage was set for controversy. At the conclusion of the bowl games, two teams emerged undefeated, but were unable to meet on the field due to the Big 10 and Pac 10's conference alignments with the Rose Bowl. Top-ranked Michigan edged seventh-ranked Washington State 21-16 in Pasadena, and No. 2 Nebraska pounded No. 3 Tennessee 42-17 in the Orange Bowl.

Following the regular season, many Associated Press voters said they would vote Michigan No. 1 if they finished the year unbeaten, regardless of how Nebraska performed. This led to a frustrating situation for Husker players and fans alike. Before and after the bowls, Nebraska quarterback Scott Frost was outspoken on the national championship scenario.

"We feel like we're getting cheated," he said prior to the Orange Bowl. "We've done everything it takes to win a national championship, and people just aren't responding to that. All we can do is win our games and concentrate on what we have to do to be a good team."

Thus, following Nebraska's decisive victory over the Volunteers, a CBS television reporter asked the Husker signal caller his thoughts on how coaches and media members should vote in their respective polls.

"If all the pollsters honestly think after watching the Rose Bowl and watching the Orange Bowl that Michigan could beat Nebraska, then go ahead and vote Michigan, by all means!" Frost shouted to the crowd of 72,000, as well as a national television audience. "But I don't think there's anybody out there that with a clear conscience can say that Nebraska, and especially [Coach] Tom Osborne, that great man, doesn't deserve a national championship for this—at least a share!"

It was a moment bred for debate; nevertheless, its ending was bittersweet for both teams, as the title was split. The Associated Press presented its award to the Wolverines while Nebraska earned the Sears Trophy from the coaches' poll. With their inability to face each other on the field, a split national championship seemed the only reconcilable solution. But what seems fair in college football doesn't work when it comes to following Christ. Jesus said, "No one can serve two masters. Either he will hate the one and love the other, or he will be devoted to the one and despise the other. You cannot serve both God and money" (Matthew 6:24).

Jesus makes it clear: no split decisions when it comes to following heavenly or earthly values. It's not just tough to serve two masters, it's impossible. The word "masters" refers to slave owners. You see, it's not like being employed and working for several people. It's the idea of giving full-time service and being totally controlled and obligated to one person. To give anything less makes the master less than a master.

We live in a society where a lot of people are materialistic and serve money. Jesus tells us He's the Master, not our credit card, not the things we have. Again, it boils down to seeing things from His perspective. It's not easy when most advertising companies are trying to make us feel inadequate and discontent about ourselves. After all, they tell us, if we just buy their product, it will solve all of our problems.

Not just money can become your master. It can be power, prestige, or trying to please other people. I repeat, anything can push its way ahead of God on your priority list. Even sports can easily become your master. I've seen it happen many times. If you let athletics squeeze out the Lord for top priority, you're wrong. You can't chase the world's dreams and honor God. Jesus said it, I didn't. So, you better make up your mind. Who's No. 1 in your life? If it's the world's values, it needs to change. One thing is for sure: God's not asking for your vote. He wants your life.

LESSON SIXTY-TWO

God's Power in You

People often tend to find self-worth in things that have nothing to do with how God values them.

Nebraska receivers' coach Ron Brown addressed this issue:

"Psalm 75:6-7 says, 'No one from the east or the west or from the desert can exalt a man. But it is God who judges: He brings one down; He exalts another.'

"Have you ever taken spiritual inventory of God's power in your life?" Brown questioned. "Every Husker football player has at least one and often more than one talent. It's important to know what that talent is and discover your role. There have been times I have asked myself, 'Am I just a mere receivers' coach in a running offense—the least prestigious position to coach?' But are these thoughts feelings or fact? The fact is: God knows exactly who you are. God thinks of you, your gifts, and your roles all the time. Rejected by man, perhaps, but accepted by God.

"He knows you like He knew Joseph—locked up and forgotten in prison. He knows you like He knew young David, feeding sheep in the wilderness. He knows you like He knew John the Baptist—alone and out of normal comforts on a mission trip. He knows you like He knew the rejected Moses, exiled in a foreign land."

Yet, God used those ordinary men and women to accomplish His purposes.

"God made Joseph not the chief leader, but the assistant to Pharaoh with enormous spiritual influence over the land. God took David from the sheep folds to kingship of a nation. God made John the Baptist significant enough to be highly honored by Jesus Himself. And God caused Moses to rebound from defeat and lead God's people from slavery in Egypt to the Promised Land.

"God has given you and me a piece of the Promised Land the moment we trusted in Jesus. Understand this, God knows how He wants you and me to claim that portion of the Promised Land.

"Take spiritual inventory of your gifts and opportunities of what God has given you right now. There's nothing Satan would want to do more to Christians than to convince them that they have little power or influence. God has created you for royalty through earthly weakness."

Did you catch what Coach Brown was saying? Your value before God has nothing to do with your circumstances or possessions. Youth and even adults often get caught up in having the right image, wearing the right brand of shoes or clothes, or saying the right things. But God has this to say about image: "So God created man in His own image, in the image of God He created him; male and female He created them" (Genesis 1:27).

This verse gives us a solid basis for true self-worth: worth that is not based on achievements, talent, or possessions; instead, worth that is based on God's ability to make us into His image. Because you bear the image of God, you can feel good about yourself. After all, cutting yourself down is criticizing God for what He has made.

Isn't it great to know God gives each of us just the right look? As people spend money to buy those right kind of clothes or cars, we need to remember that Jesus shelled out the ultimate price for you and me. He died on a wooden cross to pay the price for our sin. The immeasurable love of God and our allowing Him to work in our lives is worth far more than our earthly status and image.

LESSON SIXTY-THREE

Kicker Demonstrates Consistency

On Sept. 5, 1998, Nebraska senior kicker Kris Brown nailed a 28-yard field goal against the University of Alabama-Birmingham. The successful kick surpassed 1983 Heisman Trophy winner Mike Rozier's school record of 312 career points. The stocky four-year starter finished his Husker career with a school-record 17 consecutive field goals and 125 straight PATs. Brown finished his senior season as the seventh leading scorer in NCAA history and with the most PATs (217) in Division I history.

Kris Brown stands among the most consistently successful kickers in college football. But for any kicker, success comes at a price—it's either feast or famine. The ball either goes through the uprights or it doesn't. It's a position one plays alone. Therefore personal discipline, mental focus, and precise execution are critical. Mental preparation and toughness are every bit as important as physical conditioning.

Setting those records obviously required tremendous concentration for Kris Brown. In a similar manner, God asks us to be focused when it comes to meditating on His Word. Some think meditation just happens. Not true. Not any more than becoming good at kicking field goals happens by daydreaming. You see, meditation is not letting your mind wander all over the place. It's not chanting some meaningless phrase.

Meditation is disciplined thought, focused on Scripture for a period of time. It's like reading a text to yourself. You quietly mouth the words over and over, trying to understand each word. It's the idea of whispering or muttering to yourself. So you talk to yourself about the passage and also talk to God about it.

Meditation has been compared to how cows "chew their cud." In the morning, milk cows eat grass for several hours like a lawn mower. Later in the morning, when they start to heat up, they lie under the shade tree and begin to cough up the little balls of grass that they have swallowed. Then they re-chew the cud until they know they have all the taste out of it. Finally, they swallow it into a second stomach compartment where it is digested and processed.

Meditation on God's Word is a similar type of digestion. When you think on His Word, your mind will be filled with His thoughts and ways.

The last step in meditation is application. This step asks the question, "What do I do now?"

Psalm 119 says, "Blessed are they whose ways are blameless, who walk according to the law of the Lord. Blessed are they who keep His statutes and seek Him with all their heart. They do nothing wrong; they walk in His ways. You have laid down precepts that are to be fully obeyed" (vv. 1-4).

Kris Brown concentrates on each kick. Likewise, you need to concentrate on God's Word and ask yourself three questions: 1) What does it say? 2) What does it mean? 3) How does it apply to my life? Ask these three questions, and you'll be a can't-miss Christian on God's team.

LESSON SIXTY-FOUR

Underrated Recruits Help to Win

Every year, so-called national recruiting analysts rank what they consider to be the NCAAs' top recruiting classes. How accurate those ratings are remains questionable at best. In 1991, the Cornhusker recruiting class did not even make the top 20. And yet in 1994, those juniors and seniors of that corps of players went on to help lead NU to a consensus national championship. Starters such as center Aaron Graham, defensive tackle Christian Peter, free safety Tony Veland, outside linebacker Dwayne Harris, cornerback Barron Miles, wingback Abdul Muhammad, and quarterback Brook Berringer comprised a portion of that original list of prep recruits. Regardless of what the alleged experts thought, obviously Nebraska's coaches knew something they didn't when it came to the player-selection process that year.

Yes, that recruiting class, as well as several other Husker players, comprised the best college football team in the country in 1994. But what team had the greatest impact on the entire world? That's right; you guessed it—the team Jesus chose, the disciples.

While the Nebraska coaching staff delved into every available detail of a player's background and accomplishments so they could choose the right person, Jesus knew every detail of His team. Yes, they were a group of ordinary men and outwardly may have appeared to be a bit of a rag-tag bunch. But the Lord had called them for His special purposes.

Listen to what He said about one of His players: "I saw you while you were still under the fig tree before Philip called you" (John 1:48). Jesus was talking to Nathanael, who was shocked that Jesus knew not only his name and where he had been, but also that he was an honest man.

Jesus knows every detail of your life. Eligibility is based on God's saving grace. Nothing else. No politics. Membership to God's team is open to all who will accept Jesus Christ as Savior.

Just as high school recruits have to accept the invitation to play, so do you. God won't force you to be on His team, but He does want you to join. Here's your chance to be part of God's team. Don't be left off the team roster!

LESSON SIXTY-FIVE

Brook Berringer: A Role Model

"If you had somebody you wanted your son to be like, Brook would be a good place to start," Nebraska coach Tom Osborne stated on April 18, 1996, only short hours following former quarterback Brook Berringer's tragic death in a plane crash. "He was one of those guys who stood for all the right things. Brook was a great guy. He deserves to be remembered."

Brook Berringer was a 6'4" signal caller from Goodland, Kan., who spent the majority of his Husker career as a backup to 1995 All-American Tommie Frazier. But when Frazier was sidelined during the '94 championship run with a blood clot, Berringer started and won seven games. The determined Berringer even played a portion of the season with a punctured lung.

During the 1995 championship season, Berringer played sparingly behind Frazier. And though he possessed the ability to start almost anywhere else in the country, he never publicly complained about it. He was a team player.

"He handled a tough situation as well and with about as much dignity as anybody ever could, in terms of his playing situation," said Coach Osborne.

Berringer also gave back to the community. Whether it meant speaking at elementary schools or visiting children's hospitals, Brook Berringer defined being a role model.

I haven't met anybody yet who hasn't had some sports hero or role model. Ask people between the ages of 35-50 about their favorite player, and you're likely to find out that it was New York Yankees slugger Mickey Mantle. He was my hero, too. It doesn't seem like it was that long ago that I was collecting cards, magazines, gloves, baseballs—almost anything that had his name on it. Ask me about his statistics, and I can tell you all of his lifetime figures for home runs and batting average.

Today the heroes or role models might be Michael Jordan, Barry Sanders, or Mark McGwire. The faces have changed, but the relationships haven't. Kids and adults alike still love to watch and emulate their heroes.

A recent poll conducted by the Travelers Company showed that 37 percent of those polled selected athletes as the most positive role models. Pop artists got 14 percent and TV/movie stars got only 11 percent.

Every athlete, no matter how deserving he/she is of recognition, will never measure up to our ultimate role model: Jesus Christ. Our sports heroes will continue to struggle with the same problems all of us do. If you get to know them, you'll see that they're really no different than the rest of us. Jesus is the one hero that will never let us down.

I doubt if Jesus shows up on most polls for positive role models, but He should. How can someone who lived two thousand years ago be a positive role model? Hebrews 12:2 says, "Let us fix our eyes on Jesus, the author and perfecter of our faith . . . ."

It's time we seek Jesus as our role model and then let His light shine through us.

LESSON SIXTY-SIX

Huskers Upset No. 1 Sooners

It had been a six-year dry spell since Nebraska had beaten the University of Oklahoma, but November 11, 1978, would mark one of NU's biggest upsets in school history. With under four minutes to play, the fourth-ranked Huskers led the No. 1 Sooners 17-14. Hungry to claim the lead and a victory, OU faced third and six at the Husker 20-yard line. The play went to the nation's eventual Heisman Trophy winner, Billy Sims. Sims, eyeing the end zone, broke free for the first down and gained 17 yards—but coughed up the ball at the Nebraska three as Husker defender Jim Pillen recovered. With 3:27 remaining, Nebraska's offense gained three more first downs and ran out the clock to preserve a 17-14 win. Pandemonium broke out in Memorial stadium and across the Nebraska plains as players, coaches, and fans celebrated.

Everyone loves to see an underdog team beat the odds. And why not? They've done something remarkable, and that makes them special. Maybe that's why there is so much interest in the predictions by sportswriters. They spend hours of their time researching and studying each team so they can accurately predict the outcome of a game. The Bible also makes predictions.

Do you know what the odds are for someone fulfilling all of the prophecies that Jesus did? A prophecy is a prediction about some future event. Jesus fulfilled over three hundred Old Testament prophecies.

Now, you might argue that some of them were coincidences. Peter Stoner, using the modern science of probability, said, "That would be like taking silver dollars and laying them on the face of Texas. They will cover all of the state two feet deep. Now mark one of these silver dollars and stir the whole mass thoroughly, all over the state. Blindfold a man and tell him that he can travel as far as he wishes, but he has only one chance to pick up the marked silver dollar."

Talk about a billion-to-one. You might be thinking, "Well, that sounds pretty impressive, but so what?" I don't know about you, but I figure that if Jesus made good on that many predictions, odds are that He is who He said He was. After all, if Jesus fulfilled so many prophecies, then it only makes sense that He is who He claimed to be—the Son of God.

A "billion-in-one" chance that Jesus would fulfill over three hundred prophecies? You bet. You can also bet your life that Jesus is exactly who He says He is—the Son of God.

LESSON SIXTY-SEVEN

Coach Speaks Out on Racial Reconciliation

Nebraska receivers' coach Ron Brown is a man of bold compassion. With a heartfelt fervor, Brown champions the cause of race relations. Brown has founded six statewide Christian "I CAN" camps for disadvantaged children to attend each summer. He has also served as a Fellowship of Christian Athletes national spokesman for race reconciliation.

Ron has made the following statement in regard to race relations. "There are increasing racial tensions beginning to permeate many communities. What better opportunities for Christians to provide the healing touch in these communities than through Jesus Christ? The objective isn't to heal the races, but to heal the human heart through the love of Jesus. Races getting along should be a by-product of right Christian living."

James 2:14-26 talks about the importance of demonstrating our faith by our actions. What value is our faith if we're not living it out and honoring God by our works? If you're a Christian, can your friends, relatives, or acquaintances tell that there's something different about you? Can they see God at work in your life? Ephesians 2:8-10 explains how we are saved by faith, but are created to do good works. James 2:18b says, "I will show you my faith by what I do."

The Christian community has two extremes. One group pushes for knowledge at the expense of social action. The other group focuses almost entirely on social programs with little emphasis on Bible knowledge or sharing the gospel. Both extremes are wrong. In fact, I've learned that if Satan can't fool us with his lies, then he would like nothing better than to see us take the truth to extremes.

We need both evangelism (sharing the gospel) and social action. One without the other just doesn't work. I've heard it said, "People don't care how much you know until they know how much you care." I think that's true.

Within that same chapter of James, verses 15-16 ask what if someone is without food and clothing and you simply say, "Go, I wish you well; keep warm and be well fed." Of what value is that faith if it isn't reaching out to others in obedience to God?

Jesus put it this way, "I tell you the truth, whatever you did for one of the least of these brothers of mine, you did for me" (Matthew 25:40).

This was a parable about the importance of caring for others. The point is, we need to serve others where service is needed. He was teaching us to love and care for anyone who needs our help. A lot of us might like the government to take care of the elderly or the homeless, but God made us responsible.

How about it? What can you do to help others in need around you? What difference can you make? Maybe it's time more of us dreamed about the impact we can make for Christ by reaching out to others in need and showing people just how much we care. But be careful! Once you realize your dreams, you'll never be the same. And neither will those you help.

LESSON SIXTY-EIGHT

Booker Stifles Florida's 'Fun-and-Gun' Offense

In 1995, No. 2 Florida was eyeing a potential national title. Its biggest obstacle would be No. 1 Nebraska in the Jan. 2, 1996, Fiesta Bowl. Led by Danny Wuerffel's "fun-and-gun" passing offense, the Gators looked to exploit what they thought was Nebraska's weak link in its secondary—junior cornerback Michael Booker. But Booker met the competition head on. The speedster from Oceanside, Calif., recorded four tackles, broke up three passes, and intercepted one for a touchdown. His performance earned him the game's defensive Most Valuable Player award.

Michael Booker played mentally and physically tough against the best passing offense in the country. He rose above the competition not only because he had the physical ability to do so, but he also played with his best effort.

As Michael Booker went all out on defense to beat the competition, can a Christian go all out and be a hard-nosed competitor? Here are some athletes who believe you can be both.

"If Jesus played football, He would be the toughest player to ever play the game," said former Husker and current NFL defensive tackle John Parrella. "He would be the biggest, the fastest, and the strongest. From the snap to the whistle, He would go full speed."

Former NU All-American and present Arizona Cardinals starting center Aaron Graham has faced the most hostile battles of football on the front lines. He explained the importance of honoring God amidst fierce competition.

"Sometimes it's rough," he said, "but I draw a symbol of the cross on my wrist tape, and that gives me a chance before every play to look down at the hand that I snap the ball with and really remind myself who I'm playing for out on that field. It really helps me to stay focused in times where I might let my mouth slip. It keeps me focused on who I'm playing for."

Convinced? Well, don't take their word for it, take God's. God's Word says, "Whatever you do, work at it with all your heart, as working for the Lord, not for men." (Colossians 3:23) Did you catch the word "whatever"? This verse applies to every sport. The word "heartily" refers to giving your best effort every time. No slacking off. No taking it easy. And the motivation? For the Lord, not for your coaches, teammates, or the fans.

Convinced yet? Maybe the real question is: Do you compete allowing God to help you or do you push Him aside? Philippians 4:13 says, "I can do all things through Christ who strengthens me." God alone is our true source of strength. God wants you to lean on Him for your inner strength and compete with your maximum effort. God wants you to give your best . . . nothing more, nothing less, nothing else.

LESSON SIXTY-NINE

Fleeting Fame at the ESPY Awards

It stands among college football's classic plays of all time. It is the "Immaculate Reception" in Columbia, Mo., on Nov. 8, 1997. With No. 1 Nebraska trailing the Tigers by a touchdown and regulation time expiring, the night air is deafeningly quiet. Quarterback Scott Frost fires the ball from the 12-yard line. Husker receiver Shevin Wiggins falls backward into the end zone in slow motion, struggling to reach for the ball. In a futile effort to keep the football alive, Wiggins appears to inadvertently kick it backward. Freshman split end Matt Davison dives and clutches the football before it can touch the grass.

The reception not only propelled Nebraska to a 45-38 overtime win and eventually a share of the national title, but propelled Davison into the limelight. The split end from Tecumseh, Neb., was joined by Wiggins and Frost at ESPN's prestigious ESPY awards ceremony months later in New York City. The incredible catch received honors as the "Play of the Year."

But for Nebraska receivers' coach Ron Brown, who accompanied the trio to the awards presentation, it was an enjoyable moment, but incredibly fleeting. He explained how many people at the event were so caught up in the shallowness of outward appearance.

"At the ESPY awards, there was so much glitter and glamour," he explained. "There's so much superficiality. Even when you think of the Huskers, you think of glitter and glamour and a bunch of gladiators on a Saturday afternoon. But when you take away all the nice clothes, jewelry, and notoriety, it's going to come down to where everyone is going to spend eternity—in heaven, with streets of gold and praising God forever or in hell, burning in the lake of fire forever and ever."

The awards and status were exciting and enjoyable to experience, Brown alluded, but it bore no eternal significance and said nothing of what was truly in a person's heart.

Though people receive great praise and accolades for their accomplishments, the question is, are those deeds bearing eternal significance? Many people who are praised on this earth won't necessarily be rich in the kingdom of heaven. The Bible says pretty much the same thing in Mark 10:31: "But many who are first will be last, and the last first."

At first, this statement might sound confusing. But Jesus is clearly teaching that the values of this world will be reversed in the world to come. The idea is that those who seek only status and importance here will lose out in heaven. Those who are humble here will be great in heaven.

In sports, as in our society, we are bombarded with messages that confuse our values. The world says we should seek fame and fortune. Jesus teaches that we should seek to serve others. The rewards are different, too. While many players received their rewards here—status and prestige—the rewards in God's kingdom are not based on earthly standards, but on a commitment to Jesus and following Him faithfully.

God doesn't call us to be successful, just faithful. That's not always an easy thing to keep in focus in sports where very little is said about faithfulness. There are heavenly rewards that will be given out. Before you get excited about them, you'd better listen to what type of person will receive them.

First, those who are humble before God, who totally rely on Him, can count on a place in His kingdom. Second, those who help the needy and those who are hurting will receive much comfort in their own lives. Third, those who are gentle, yet strong and with self control will win out. Fourth, those who are excited about righteousness, both heavenly and earthly, will receive from the Lord personal contentment and satisfaction.

If this list sounds familiar, it should. Each of these rewards and character traits is based on four of the eight Beatitudes found in the Bible. God honors certain character traits and gives us particular rewards for each. Some of these rewards we'll see here and now; some we'll get later in heaven. One thing you can be sure of . . . God cares more about faithfulness to Him than success that depends on this world.

LESSON SEVENTY

Miami's Trash-Talking Sapp Grows Weary

Miami's 1994 Lombardi Award-winning defensive tackle Warren Sapp was as feisty a trash talker as he was a dominating force on the front lines. During the Jan. 1, 1995, Orange Bowl, the swaggering bull jeered and talked smack to opposing Husker players. But the Huskers' physical play gradually wore out the home team. By fourth quarter, Nebraska's two-yard runs became eight-yarders as the 'Canes were playing back on their heels.

"It was loud and hostile," former NU free safety Tony Veland described the Orange Bowl atmosphere. "[But] I don't think they were used to the style of football we play: four quarters of smashmouth football. And consequently, by the time the fourth quarter came, they really didn't have anything left."

Thus, symbolically, on first and ten from the Miami 14 with 2:46 remaining, NU fullback Cory Schlesinger exploded up the middle past Miami's main trash talker for the winning touchdown. Sapp's strength was zapped.

Talking trash is nothing new. It's been a part of sports for years, but it seems to be getting more media attention. Most of the talk seems harmless, like current NBA star Shaquille O'Neal's remark to an opponent when he was an All-American at Louisiana State.

He said, "I don't care how good you play. I'm still going to be the No. 1 draft pick."

The other player's response was, "I thought about saying something back, but then I realized he was right."

The tongue is small but powerful. In the Bible, James refers to the tongue as a fire's spark. As explosive as Nebraska's national championship offenses were, so much more is the tongue. If most of us are honest, we've probably talked a little trash ourselves. Sports has a way of bringing out both the best and the worst in us. Listen to what the Bible says about the power of the tongue to influence and destroy:

"The tongue is a fire . . . a restless evil and full of deadly poison" (James 3:6, 8).

No doubt about it, the tongue can do a lot of good or a lot of damage. Does God really care if we take a shot at someone else?

Listen to what King David said in Psalm 39:1: "I will watch my ways and keep my tongue from sin; I will put a muzzle on my mouth."

Good advice. Another book in the Bible, Proverbs, is a good book to study if you want to know more about the power of our words. In fact, the terms tongue, lips, and mouth appear 150 times in this book about wisdom.

If anyone had a reason to talk trash, it had to be Jesus. As Jesus was slandered, beaten, and crucified, He remained silent. He didn't lash out at those who had wronged Him. He left the situation in God's hands. And so should we.

Tempted to let somebody have it? Caught in the grind of trash talk? Now is a good time to stop. Trust me, you'll never regret leaving the trash talk where it belongs.